THE RISE OF THE NEW EAST

THE RISE OF THE NEW EAST

BUSINESS STRATEGIES FOR SUCCESS IN A WORLD OF INCREASING COMPLEXITY

BEN SIMPFENDORFER

palgrave
macmillan

THE RISE OF THE NEW EAST
Copyright © Ben Simpfendorfer, 2014.

First published in 2014 by
PALGRAVE MACMILLAN®
in the U.S.—a division of St. Martin's Press LLC,
175 Fifth Avenue, New York, NY 10010.

Where this book is distributed in the UK, Europe and the rest of the world,
this is by Palgrave Macmillan, a division of Macmillan Publishers Limited,
registered in England, company number 785998, of Houndmills,
Basingstoke, Hampshire RG21 6XS.

Palgrave Macmillan is the global academic imprint of the above companies
and has companies and representatives throughout the world.

Palgrave® and Macmillan® are registered trademarks in the United States,
the United Kingdom, Europe and other countries.

ISBN: 978–1–137–37005–1

Library of Congress Cataloging-in-Publication Data:

Simpfendorfer, Ben.
    The rise of the new East : business strategies for success in a world of
increasing complexity / Ben Simpfendorfer.
        pages cm
    ISBN 978–1–137–37005–1 (hardback)
        1. East Asia—Commerce. 2. South Asia—Commerce. 3. East Asia—
Foreign economic relations. 4. South Asia—Foreign economic relations.
5. East Asia—Economic conditions—21st century. 6. South Asia—Economic
conditions—21st century. I. Title.

HF3820.5.Z5S56 2014
330.95—dc23   2014014605

A catalogue record of the book is available from the British Library.

Design by Newgen Knowledge Works (P) Ltd., Chennai, India.

First edition: June 2014

10 9 8 7 6 5 4 3 2 1

Printed in the United States of America.

To Julia, Alex, and Lucas

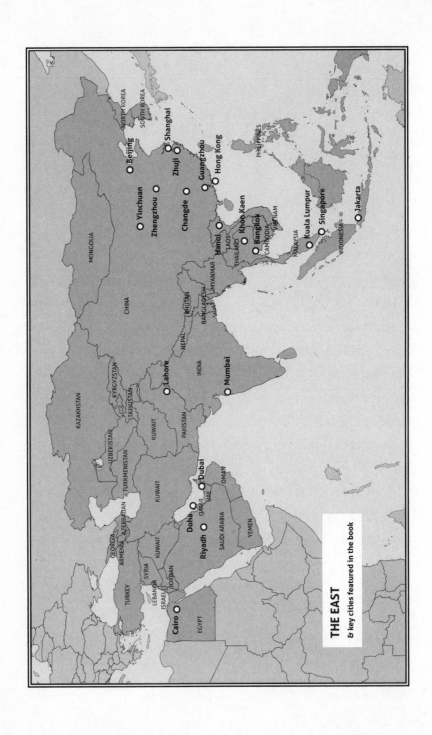

THE EAST
& key cities featured in the book

CONTENTS

ACKNOWLEDGMENTS

MANY THANKS TO ALL THOSE INTERVIEWED FOR THE BOOK OR who assisted in its creation: Alwi Aidid, Colin Airdrie, Tayseer al Khayat, Amira al Misry, Mohammed Al Sudairi, Anson Bailey, Roger Ball, Teresa Barger, Tanaaz Bhatia, Jonathan Bonsey, Sundar Burra, Rob Cain, Nandini Chopra, Daniel de Blocq van Scheltinga, David Eldon, Michael Every, Matthew Flynn, Terry Foecke, Michael Friedlander, David Fullbrook, Rami Ghandour, Yusuf Hatia, Helmuth Hennig, Craig Hope-Johnstone, Julia Hung, Wenna Hung, Shilpa Jamkhandikar, Hartono Jap, Ivy Ji, Man Jit Singh, Datuk Hamzah Kassim, Parag Khanna, Roger King, Simon Kitchen, Payal Kothari, Alex Lee, Cherry Leong, Diajeng Lestari, Lewis Leung, David Li, Jason Lo, Ringo Mak, Alice Martell, Kenneth Mays, Noha Medhat, Sara Menguc, Tom Miles, Gideon Milstein, Sarah Monks, Daniel Morler, Tony Munroe, Zarina Nalla, Frank Newman, Tony Ngai, Soren Nikolajsen, Neale O'Connor, Tamsine O'Riordan, Glen Plumbridge, Wasant Pothipimpanon, Wendi Putranto, Christophe Roussel, Omar Shaikh, Tariq Shaikh, Josef Sheikh, Tony Shi, Ralph Simpfendorfer, Angkana Songvejkasem, Paul Speltz, Salman Tariq, Jehil Thakkar, Richard Thomas, Gautam Verma, Aseena Viccajee, Thibault Villet, Widi Widiana, Simon Williams, Cindy Wong, Michael Wykoff, Achmed Zaky, Edge Zarrella, James Zhang, Raymond Zhou, and Ernst Zimmermann.

INTRODUCTION

TAKE A LOOK AT THE EAST: IT IS CHANGING FAST. NOT ONLY IS THE region growing, it is also evolving in unexpected ways: Chinese shoppers are going online to buy clothing and shoes at rates unheard of in America or Europe; American film studios are producing films alongside local partners in Hindi and Tamil; Hong Kong jewelry companies are opening more stores in a single country than the high-end American jeweler Tiffany & Co. operates globally; foreign retail multinationals are switching from hypermarkets to small-format stores as they chase Thailand's upcountry shoppers.

The idea that the East is rising is not new. However, straight-line trajectories are pure fantasy, as a growing number of influences shape the region's fortunes. For a long time, the East was manufacturing and selling goods to the West, and making good money in the process. But the rise of domestic markets is creating new opportunities for local and foreign companies alike, even if the differences between markets are significant. The expansion of cross-border trade and investment is also changing the region's outlook as local companies look to their neighbors for new sources of growth.

The underlying theme of this book is that the East is growing but also growing in complexity. In my conversations with multinationals and smaller companies, I hear similar conversations across sectors and countries: the region offers more opportunities than ever, but it also presents more challenges.

Why is this? The East's $18,700 billion economy is certainly a vast market, but consider how cultures, tastes, incomes, and regulations differ between even some of its larger economies, such as China, India, Korea, Indonesia, and Saudi Arabia. Moreover, the fact that growth is spreading more evenly across the region, from capital cities to midsized and even smaller cities, means that companies are having to build out a bigger footprint than ever. Having a factory in Guangzhou, or a few retail stores in Hong Kong and Singapore might have been sufficient in the 1990s and the first decade of the 2000s, but it isn't sufficient today.

Moreover, the region is adapting fast. I have spent nearly 20 years living in the East, and the change over the past ten years has been particularly stunning. In part, that is a natural outcome of economic development. But the ability of consumers and companies to jump online and check out what is happening in the rest of the world has accelerated the pace of change. Local consumers are increasingly demanding a quality and variety of products similar to those available in the West, and local companies are observing their foreign competitors' best practices, then adapting them to local conditions, thus providing a stiff challenge to firms in the region.

The importance of the change cannot be overstated. In the past, most CEOs and other senior executives were able to manage in the region with a good "mental map," meaning that they could make sensible decisions based on their own understanding of how the region operated. But the growing complexity of business means this is no longer possible. Most no longer have a "mental map" that is big enough to evaluate the opportunities between midsized Chinese and Indian towns, for instance, or the risks of rising minimum wages for factories in Indonesia and Bangladesh. Instead, they increasingly have to rely on their country managers and local staff.

Of course, the extra information is helpful. But it also adds an extra layer of complexity, and even a home bias. For instance, it is understandable if a country manager in China or India should argue the case for investing in their own retail network or manufacturing facilities: we all want to succeed.

Linkages between sectors add an additional layer of complexity. This book deliberately tackles a range of subjects in order to draw links between them. Whether urbanization results in livable productive cities will determine how much consumers are able to spend, and how they spend; the vulnerability of the region's inland logistics chains will impact how companies produce in the region and sell to their consumers; the growing importance of local content to the entertainment industry is a similar challenge to that faced by industrial multinationals struggling to localize and simultaneously stay global.

For that reason, this book is not an exhaustive review of the East's opportunities and challenges, but instead a snapshot. It is a review limited to my own conversations traveling across the region for work and is due to my good fortune in being able to speak with people at the leading edge of change in their industry.

This book focuses on the East, which I define as a region that spreads from Beijing to Istanbul, includes almost 50 countries, and is home to over half the world's population. It is a region that includes countries such as China, Vietnam, Thailand, India, Saudi Arabia, and Syria, among others. Of course, these countries are all technically part of the Asian continent. However, in practice, the word "Asia" is used to refer to a much smaller region stopping at India. And so I stick to that practice in the book, using the word "Asia" to refer to the countries that make up principally East Asia and South Asia.

I would add two exceptions to my definition of the East. The first is that I focus on developing or newly developed countries, so I do not include Japan. Not only would the country's inclusion skew much of the data, but it is also at a very different stage of development. I also include Egypt in the story. Though the country lies on the African continent, it is very much engaged with the East, whether through its Muslim population, historical ties to the Middle East, growing trade ties to East Asia, or the fact that the 2011 overthrow of Mubarak has inspired others in the East to protest.

Why focus on the East? For a start, simply looking at Asia is increasingly too narrow a focus when considering the region's commercial opportunities and challenges. For instance, India's ties to Kuwait, Saudi Arabia, and the United Arab Emirates are far stronger than those to China, Hong Kong, or Thailand. There is also a strong case to argue that a business manager in Singapore, for instance, might have regional responsibility for a company's operations in Dubai. But it would be tough for the same manager to argue for responsibility over a firm's business in Johannesburg or Rio de Janeiro.

The Muslim consumer is also a religious and commercial anchor for the region. Some 80 percent of the world's Muslim population lives in the region. That means 1.1 billion Muslim consumers who are typically young, online, and increasingly ready to spend. In response, Islamic banks are rolling out regional platforms in Dubai; multinationals are building halal food-processing facilities in Kuala Lumpur; and even China's Communist Party has seen the opportunities in developing its own halal-compliant industries. For firms looking for the next big thing, the Muslim consumer ticks the right boxes.

Trade flows within the region are also growing. In fact, over 50 percent of Saudi Arabia's oil exports are currently sold to Asia, especially to China and Korea, and the latter's reliance on the Middle East for its energy needs will only bind the two regions more tightly together.[1] Of course, Asia still sells primarily to America, Europe, and neighboring

Asian countries. Still, the Middle East is a bigger market than either Sub-Saharan Africa or Latin America. Asia is also increasingly using the Middle East as a stepping-stone to Africa, to the benefit of Dubai and other business hubs.

However, to think of the region as an economic bloc would also be a mistake. My last book, *The New Silk Road*, focused on the return of the historical trade route. The term leaves us with the idea that traders once traveled smoothly along the road, buying jade or silks in China's Xian, and then transporting them to Syria, Turkey, and even Europe. Far from it. The evidence suggests that few traders actually traveled far from their hometowns; even then they returned quickly. It was goods, rather than people, that traveled along the road, as they were passed from trader to trader, making the Silk Road look more like a complex web of commercial activity rather than the single route of popular imagination.

The region looks much the same today. There is no single trend, or new Silk Road, that can point to the region's future, but instead hundreds of daily interactions between people, companies, and countries that are pushing the region forward in unexpected ways and, in turn, creating commercial opportunities.

That said, China is central to many of the region's biggest changes, and a large share of the book focuses on the country for that reason. Not only does China account for almost half of the East's total economic output, but the country's rising wage costs are also reshaping global manufacturing chains; a booming e-commerce business is leading the region, if not the world; water shortages in the northern regions are on a par with those in the Middle East; and, lastly, China has more increasingly affluent consumers spread across more cities than any other country in the world.

The chapters aren't necessarily meant to be read in order. The opening chapter on the rise of the region's consumers is central to many of the changes described in the book because this rise is the source of stronger domestic markets. However, each chapter is intended to capture a key issue that will both impact those operating in the region and have side effects for other countries and sectors, such as the impact of the region's rising domestic demand on the logistics industry. Even the entertainment industry offers lessons for others as it faces stronger local competition.

The conclusion ties the messages from each chapter together, attempting to build a "mental map" for readers. Indeed, it is this spillover between countries and sectors that makes the East so exciting and an increasingly difficult place to pin down. And understanding how a change in one country or sector may ripple throughout the region will eventually become an important part of any business manager or policy maker's toolbox. The East is also changing so fast that any decent "map" needs regular live updates; I will continue to comment on those changes through other channels, including editorials, social media, and website updates.

1

THE RISE OF THE EAST'S MIDDLE CLASS

SELLING TO THE REGION'S NEW CONSUMERS

HARTONO JAP LEANS FORWARDS IN HIS CHAIR TO TELL HIS STORY. "I asked the hotel developer, who are your target clients? Who wants to stay in a hotel that is far from the beach? In fact, it's not even near the beach, but in Bali's business and commercial area." He pauses before continuing. "Then I visited two years later and the hotel was full. But not with foreigners. It was full of middle-class Indonesian tourists who didn't mind traveling back and forth to the beach each day on buses or in cars, as well as some middle-level professionals on business trips. Brilliant! This was a real success story."[1]

Jap was a banker at the time and was assessing whether to give the developer a loan. In the end, the hotel was fully occupied and profitable. The owner had benefited from the rise in domestic tourism as Indonesia's increasingly affluent middle class started to spend its wealth and wanted to visit Bali—no different from foreign tourists. But rather than travel by plane, many traveled by bus and ferry to the island. They were also happy to stay in cheaper hotels away from the beach. They had growing purchasing power, just not enough yet to stay at the island's more expensive five-star hotels.

The rise of Indonesia's consumers has captured the attention of multinationals, and understandably so—from beaches to biscuits, consumers are shopping. The world's fourth most populous country was always going to be one of great opportunities and, finally, the country appears to be delivering as promised.

In Jakarta, the country's capital, consumers are increasingly tempted by a growing range of premium products from shampoos to foreign beers. Unilever, the Anglo-Dutch consumer goods multinational, has seen its annual sales more than double in five years to $290 million.[2] Honda, the Japanese motorcycle manufacturer, similarly saw its sales double to over 4 million units during the same period. Meanwhile, traveling salesmen fill the country's growing number of budget hotels, from Fave to POP! to HARRIS, marketing their goods and tapping into the growing number of affluent consumers.

For the city's wealthier residents, car ownership is also rising rapidly. Passenger car sales doubled in five years to 850,000, making the country a larger car market than either Australia or Spain and likely to shortly overtake the United Kingdom.[3] Jakarta's sprawling low-rise suburbs and the municipal government's failure to invest in road and rail infrastructure result in suffocating traffic. But, for the city's residents, multi-hour commutes in slow-moving traffic are a visible sign of having joined the expanding ranks of middle-class households.

As a former China economist, I see that Indonesia's consumer boom shares many similarities to that of China over the past two decades. China has already seen huge growth in sales of premium beers and shampoos, as well as rapid expansion of the country's budget hotels, such as Home Inn or Motel 168. Indonesia's auto sales have also flourished at almost the same point they did in China when GDP per capita crossed $4,000. And, of course, many Chinese cities are suffocated by similar traffic jams, although the country's rapidly expanding subway networks do at least offer an alternative to road rage.

Jap has the right idea. Educated in the United States and Singapore, he returned to his home country in 1995 to ride Indonesia's robust growth. Working in a number of senior positions for international banks across the region, he eventually joined a local leasing and financing company as Vice CEO. He is a generous host as we eat together at Ocha & Bella, an Italian restaurant at the Morrissey Hotel. I ask if this is it, the moment Indonesia's consumers really emerge. "Yes," he answers. "With more than half the population below the age of 30 years, the consumer story will be hot for the next 20 to 30 years."

The rise of China's consumers was already a powerful story. But the notion of another 240 million Indonesians gradually joining them is also persuasive. Together, they are the world's first and fourth most populous countries and are finally, and justifiably, emerging as important sources of global growth. There will be bumps in the road and periods of slow growth or rising inflation; indeed, Indonesia was facing such a bump in the autumn of 2013. But as Jap argues, it is the next 20 to 30 years that companies are banking on in Indonesia—as well as in China and the rest of the East.

THE SHEER SIZE OF THE EAST'S CONSUMER CLASSES DAZZLES. IT'S NO surprise really, given that the region accounts for 50 percent of the world's population. But the numbers make for a wonderful set of PowerPoint slides as management teams try to convince their executive boards to invest in more retail outlets, bigger sales and distribution networks, and larger marketing teams.

I spent much of 2013 crunching numbers to measure the region's middle classes. It isn't a straightforward calculation. The middle class is generally measured by household income, but the problem is that tax collection isn't widespread in many developing countries, which leaves economists trying to aggregate a mix of income measures from a variety of countries. It's all very messy. To make the problem worse, there's no real agreement on who "is" and "isn't" middle class, so economists and consultants alike fall back on a range of terms, such as "mass affluent" or "upper aspirants."

Regardless of the difficulty in concretely defining the middle class, the results are stunning. In 2013, I estimated the number of households earning more than $15,000 per year, adjusted for purchasing-power parity, at 400 million. Of those, half were in China and the remainder split evenly across the rest of the region. The number of households earning $25,000 per year was a lower but still sizeable 150 million, again with the majority in China.[4]

But it's when the figures are applied to specific products that we see really impressive results. Here is an example: the number of automobiles sold in the East reached an estimated 24 million in 2012,[5] meaning that the region's car market was almost twice the size of the US market the same year.[6] If each country were to record a 5 percent growth rate in automobile sales over the coming years, the figure would reach around 36 million by 2020. And for those who don't believe in straight-line trajectories, sales growth at even half that rate would still result in sales of 30 million by the same year.

Auto sales are a popularly cited number as they are easily measured. For other products, analysts can derive figures based on economic and industry data, and it is easy to arrive at stratospheric figures even when applying some relatively conservative assumptions. For instance, the cosmetic and beauty product industry in the United States was worth around $60 billion in 2012, or 0.5 percent of total household consumption.[7] Assuming that sales account for just 0.2 percent of household consumption in the East by 2020, the region's cosmetic sales are expected to hit $40 billion the same year. And, by 2030, they may well reach $70 billion.[8]

At this point, however, the story does go horribly off track. Yes, the region's consumption is large. But it is also spread across nearly 50 countries, each with different cultural tastes, customs barriers, and national currencies, to name just a few challenges. What sells in Jakarta won't necessarily sell in Beijing.

Compare this to the rise of the mighty American consumer from the 1950s until the recent global financial crisis. During those six decades, American consumers accounted for around one-sixth of global growth, an astonishing feat.[9] They also supercharged growth for what are now some of the world's largest consumer product companies: Kellogg's, Procter & Gamble, and Mars Confectionery. Many others also benefited from being able to sell to a fast-growing single market. Those same companies must look back fondly at the opportunity to sell to a market where everyone spoke the same language, settled in the same currency, and had generally similar cultural tastes.

Not so in Asia. The size of the region's middle classes might dazzle, but so will its complexity. The same American consumer product companies have to not only sell across nearly 50 countries, but also set up retail outlets, sales and distribution, and marketing teams across a larger number of cities within each country. The region has more than 325 cities with populations greater than 750,000, as compared to just 59 in the United States. It is a complexity that will also assist local competitors who are more nimble at adapting to local tastes, who don't face customs barriers, and who are dealing with a single currency.

And that's just the beginning. The income disparities are also significant. Indeed, the talk about a middle class in China and Indonesia can be misleading as purchasing power in the two countries is materially different even if consumer product multinationals are making good money in both countries.

Again, we dug into the data and pulled out dozens of series on household income brackets and average salaries across the two countries. In China, the wealthiest 40 percent of urban households are earning more than $10,000 per year, although the actual figures vary widely by city and among top earners.[10] In Indonesia, by contrast, the threshold for the wealthiest 40 percent of urban households was around $3,500. Certainly the top 5 percent of Indonesian households take home big salaries, but most of the country's so-called middle-class consumers have significantly less purchasing power than do members of the middle class in China.[11]

IF INDONESIA OFFERS GREAT PROMISE, THEN CHINA IS ALREADY DELIVERING thanks to those higher incomes. Yet, the challenges are also greater as the country's shoppers are spread more widely: China has 143 cities with a population larger than 750,000 compared to 15 in Indonesia, making China a blueprint for complexity.[12]

Even the big Chinese retail and restaurant chains often focus on only parts of the country rather than blanketing every city with outlets. Take Peacebird, a local apparel chain with 922 stores in over 150 cities. Nearly one-quarter of those stores are in Zhejiang province, while neighboring Jiangsu and Anhui provinces account for another quarter. Or consider Little Sheep, a local hotpot chain that operates 376 restaurants in 121 cities. Nearly half the restaurant chain's outlets are located in just five provinces, including Guangdong and Zhejiang in the south and Beijing, Hebei, and Shandong in the north.

The city of Zhengzhou has Peacebird and Little Sheep outlets. It lies about 300 miles from the coast in China's heartland. It is a harsh city with few public parks, and it is covered in a permanent haze of pollution and construction dust as the developers build vast new commercial and residential districts. The local zoo is packed on a weekend for lack of options. But Zhengzhou is also the capital of Henan province and the commercial focal point for 90 million people, making it similar in size to Thailand or the Philippines. The city itself is home to 3 million people and growing rapidly as its gravitational pull attracts rural residents and former coastal factory workers.

Zhengzhou is a long way from Beijing or Shanghai, but if you're shopping for a Dyson vacuum cleaner, then the flagship store of Zhengzhou's biggest retailer, Dennis, is a good place to start. The retailer's flagship store is over 15 stories tall and is built at the intersection of Huayuan Road and Nongye Road. It looms over its neighbors and brings to mind the grand commercial stores constructed by Harrods in London or Saks in New York a century earlier when retailers were bringing a new shopping experience to the masses. Inside, the store is all polished floors, bright lights, and attractive design. It's also full of shoppers.

Here, on the twelfth floor, is one of Dyson's two Zhengzhou outlets. Of course, Dyson's products aren't cheap. The British household appliance maker is famed for its engineering and ability to improve on commonly used household electrical goods. The company's founder, James Dyson, initially started out by adapting technology used in sawmills to create the first vacuum cleaner that didn't lose suction. More recently it is the company's bladeless fans, large circular rings pumping out a steady stream of air, that have caught the world's attention, including that of Chinese shoppers.

"We only opened three months ago," said the saleswoman proudly as she handed over a brochure. I remark on the sticker price of $750 for a vacuum cleaner and she quickly points out that "Zhengzhou's prices will always be higher after you add duty and logistics costs. We have to ship the goods a long way, after all," she said.

Fair enough. But are they selling? "Yes, at least 20 units a week," she replied confidently.

Now, a saleswoman might have an incentive to inflate her weekly sales in front of a customer. But Dyson understandably sees China as a big opportunity. By the spring of 2013, the company had opened up over 40 outlets across the country in first- and second-tier cities, and the company had planned to open at least 220 by the winter of 2013. Having initially delayed its market entry, Dyson subsequently faced a vastly larger, but also more complicated market. Opening up in just Beijing, Shanghai, or Guangzhou might have worked a decade ago, but not today, as Chinese household purchasing power has risen across the country and is no longer limited to just a few major coastal cities.

Helmuth Hennig, CEO of Jebsen & Co., has contributed to Dyson's expansion. The company has a rich history as a more than 100-year-old Hong Kong–based trading house, marketing and distributing high-end products in China and the rest of the region for a range of clients from Robert Mondavi wines to Raymond Weil watches. Hennig himself has lived in Hong Kong for the past 30 years, working for most of that time at Jebsen, where he has sold consumer goods to Chinese households that might once have aspired to own a bicycle or a sewing machine, but today are increasingly likely to prefer a Swiss-made watch or a British-designed bagless vacuum cleaner.

It would be easy for Hennig to be optimistic given the changes he has witnessed. But he is instead reassuringly pragmatic as he lists the

challenges for foreign brand owners. "The market has changed funda-
mentally in the past decade," he says from his offices high above Hong
Kong's busy Causeway Bay. "It wasn't so long ago that we sold only
through the government-owned Friendship Stores in just a few big cities. But Chinese consumers are spoilt for choice today. Even some of
the big foreign luxury brands are suffering stagnant sales in their existing stores, as consumers look elsewhere."[13]

He ticks off those challenges. "Product availability is critical. If we
sell in just a few cities, then we only stoke consumer interest and attract
copycats in the cities where we don't have stores. That's why Dyson has
to tap into each opportunity and make its product available across even
midsized cities.

"Local competition is another growing threat. Think of your everyday products, such as toothpaste or washing powder. Sure, the foreign
brands initially made some big gains in the wealthier cities. But they
are having to work with local brands in order to penetrate the mid- and
small-sized cities. Local competitors are also offering an increasingly
comparable product and so consumers are overwhelmed for choice.
That's less true for high-end products, but even here there are growing
challenges."

A quick walk around the household appliance section on the
twelfth floor of Dennis illustrates his point: the floor is full of high-end
American and European products mixed up with mainly low-cost local
versions. Local shoppers have numerous choices, and the department
store is unsurprisingly busy.

It's not just the foreign consumer product companies that are challenged, but also the retailers themselves. Dennis is Zhengzhou's largest
retailer with 13 department stores and hypermarkets in the city districts. The city also has foreign retailers, but just four Walmarts and
three Carrefours. Even as the big foreign retailers were expanding in

China's larger coastal cities, Dennis was observing and copying, and by the time the foreign retailers noticed Zhengzhou, Dennis was already a robust competitor. The retailer's owners not only understand local preferences, but also presumably enjoy strong relations with local officials and so will be difficult to compete with.

Still, that's good news for Dyson as it looks to tap into local demand. Having listed the challenges, Hennig then ticks off the solutions. "You need to understand what sells in each region; you need to create a national training school for staff; you need to think about how to fabricate a standard shop display," he says. "None of these are straightforward given the scale of the operations." But they certainly might appear familiar to Dyson's British-based employees who likely use similar strategies to sell the firm's products at home, an indication of how China's consumer market is growing in numbers and in purchasing power, but also growing in sophistication much as markets did in the West.

THAT SAME NIGHT I WAS TO CATCH A FLIGHT BACK TO SHENZHEN, BUT THE flight was canceled, and then a subsequent flight was delayed. But that's business as usual in today's China and also the source of many flight-rage videos on the country's version of YouTube. It's also one more reason that selling into the country's second-tier cities can be so exhausting. Thibault Villet understands just how tiring it can be. Villet was previously head of luxury sales in China for the French cosmetics company L'Oréal and spent much of his time on a plane traveling to those smaller cities across the country in order to speak with staff and check that the right product was on sale in the right locations.

Villet still sells to those same cities, but when I ask him when he was last on a plane, he replies with a satisfied smile, "It was six months ago that I last left Shanghai."

Villet is now co-founder and CEO of Glamour-Sales China, an online flash sales retailer of luxury goods. Established in 2010, the company is part of a rapidly evolving e-commerce sector that is changing the way China's retailers engage with the country's consumers, especially in medium-sized cities such as Zhengzhou. I met with Villet on a hot and sticky summer day in 2013 at his office in Shanghai's Huangpu district. From the meeting room you can see some of the firm's 110 staff busy behind their PCs. Villet notes there are another 40 at a warehouse a short drive away. I ask how many are based outside Shanghai. "None," he replies.[14]

That's a stunning response. Not only does Villet rarely travel outside of Shanghai, but all of his staff work within the city. And yet over 30 percent of the company's sales are to second-tier Chinese cities, much like Zhengzhou, and around 30 percent to even smaller third- and fourth-tier cities.

In fact, the firm sells to customers in over 1,000 Chinese cities, all without having to deal with a department store such as Dennis. And after sweating in Zhengzhou exploring the city's department stores and suffering canceled flights, I can appreciate the attraction of selling to Chinese consumers in hundreds of small- to medium-sized cities from the comfort of an air-conditioned office in downtown Shanghai. It's also a major attraction for a firm like Glamour-Sales that only has to deal with a single set of municipal party chiefs, tax officials, and regulators (a big bonus in China).

Glamour-Sales is one of several flash retailers in China adapting a business model first developed in France in the early 2000s: online flash retailers negotiate discounts from brands carrying excess stocks and then offer the products to a list of clients in an online sale lasting just a few days. In the case of Glamour-Sales, the firm sells goods on behalf of over 660 mainly high-end foreign brands. The company's home page offers a feast of discounted goods—Steve Madden shoes, HOM underwear, DVF dresses, Diesel jeans, and Dolce & Gabbana bags. Most goods are sold at a discount of between 40 percent and 70 percent. I signed up as one of the company's 2.4 million members and immediately started receiving alerts on my iPhone.

However, while the business model might not be new to either the West or the East, the way the Chinese have taken to e-commerce is shaking up the global retail sector. "You wouldn't believe how they are buying," Villet says as he opens up his MacBook Air and walks me through a recent survey by an American market research group. The results show that 46 percent of urban Chinese have purchased footwear products online in the past three months, compared to just 18 percent of Americans and 18 percent of Europeans. For clothing and accessories, the figures are 58 percent of Chinese, 38 percent of Americans, and 34 percent of Europeans.

These are differences that make a mockery of emerging and developed world classifications. Who is really emerging and who is developed? Much of the change can be attributed to the country's 190 million 25- to 35-year-olds. It is this age group that accounts for 50 percent of the company's total members. This is a generation that has generally only known good times. The last growth slowdown was in the late 1990s when most of these consumers were just 10 to 20 years old, but since then China's economic growth has averaged 10 percent and inflation just 2 percent.

It's no wonder they are spending. And that excites Edge Zarrella. He is China Clients and Innovation Partner for KPMG, one of the world's Big Four auditors, after spending eight years as the firm's Global Partner in charge of IT Advisory. "I get sick of being asked when China will produce its own Steve Jobs. That's the wrong question," he says over lunch at Hong Kong's China Club, itself established by one of Hong Kong's more entrepreneurial businessmen, Sir David Tang. "China is already innovating," continues Zarrella. "But it's the Chinese consumer who is innovating in the way they are buying."[15]

Zarrella is popularly described as KPMG's rock star, and he certainly doesn't look like a typical auditor. Wearing his hair shoulder length, Zarrella looks as if he would be more comfortable with a guitar strung across his back as he bounces around onstage asking challenging questions of his audience. We catch up shortly after he finished a series of events in Beijing, Shanghai, and Hong Kong to launch KPMG's new publication, *The Changing Face of Commerce*. The report includes a single killer statistic that explains why China's e-commerce sector was turning retail in the country upside down.

"The average Chinese has three to five smart devices—smartphones, tablets, e-readers. The average American has just one to two and the average German less than one," says Zarrella. "In fact, when I put the question to a group of CEOs in Shanghai recently, they each had an average six to seven devices.

"But it's not just how many devices you own. It's what we are doing with these devices that matters," he continues. "And in China, we are buying. It's also not just China. In Indonesia, we are buying. In Malaysia, we are buying. The West doesn't get the scale of the commercial revolution taking place over here. But would you believe that Asia's online payments transactions are now worth twice the combined value of transactions in America and Europe? The problem is that most multinationals are still only asking what Asian consumers are buying, rather than how they are buying."

Of course, none of this would be possible without a robust infrastructure to support China's growing online business. And both Villet and Zarrella are quick to recognize the improvements. Villet offers two specific reasons that help explain why Glamour-Sales has done so well in China in just a few years.

The first is payments systems. "It's amazing to see how fast they improved," he says. Today, over 70 percent of the firm's payments are made online, rather than by cash on delivery. The figures were the reverse just two years ago. Most are made through Alipay, the online payments system owned by B2B giant Alibaba and a leader in its field. The regulators are helping the industry's evolution. A few years ago they required approval for transactions of just 500 yuan ($80). Today, shoppers are spending nearly $10,000 with Glamour-Sales without needing approval.

Then there is the logistics network. Glamour-Sales delivers its goods by express freight to addresses in Shanghai in 24 hours, to Beijing in 48 hours, and to most other addresses across the country in three days. The Shenzhen-based express air freight courier company, SF Express, is one of the more visible beneficiaries of the industry change, shipping a share of the $160 billion sold on Taobao, China's version of eBay, each year.[16] The firm's SF-branded trucks and express packages are now a standard sight in China and Hong Kong, and increasingly in the rest of Asia, with the firm having opened six country offices since 2008.[17]

So should Dyson simply sell its products online, rather than opening 220 outlets? Indeed, Dyson already offers most of its products to British shoppers through its English-language online store. And if an online strategy made more sense, then could any foreign brand owner sell to Chinese consumers without even setting up in China?

I put the question to Villet. "Yes and no," he replies. "We have the power to launch new brands through direct emails to our members or through social media channels, such as Weibo or WeChat, and around 10 percent of our products are in fact new brands." Yet Glamour-Sales also benefits from the fact that the large share of the company's brands already have stores in China: for instance, Steve Madden has 57 stores in 27 cities; Diesel has 31 stores in 21 cities; and Louis Vuitton has 47 stores in 32 cities.

In this, China is little different from the rest of the world with shoppers wanting to view an item in the store before actually buying it. Perhaps a shopper might choose to buy a Dyson vacuum cleaner online, but only after first testing the real thing in one of the company's stores. Most importantly, it also allows Dyson to demonstrate the quality of its product against inevitable cheaper copycats. (And copycat Dyson bladeless fans are certainly easy to spot across China.) In that case, retail outlets are needed across more cities, but fewer in number in each city.

What makes the China model so exciting is whether it is replicable. Take Indonesia, with an estimated 55 million Facebook users, as an example.[18] Mobile penetration rates are around 80 percent and smartphones account for one in four phones sold. From Hong Kong, I find myself reaching out to contacts across the region through LinkedIn, and Indonesia always stands out for the sheer number of contacts with accounts and the speed at which they reply to invitation requests. Online networking is perhaps an antidote to the country's traffic jams that can result in bladder-bursting trips between meetings.

Most important, though, is the way that retailers may be able to access Indonesia's consumers through their smart devices, allowing them to shop for goods online. That would be a major advantage for any firm trying to sell to a huge population in a country made up of a chain of islands around 3,000 miles in length, wider than Australia. If Dyson can open an outlet in Zhengzhou, why not Surabaya? Shoppers might then place their order online, allowing firms to hold most of their stock in a single city, rather than worry about inventory management across multiple stores in multiple cities on multiple islands.

The obstacle, of course, is logistics. Indonesia's road networks are improving, but they simply aren't comparable to China's multilane highways and integrated logistics hubs. Moreover, only 60 percent of the population lives on Java, the country's main island, with the remainder spread across the archipelago, thus requiring a combination of road, sea, and air transport. Even on Java there are challenges, as the country has few midsized modern trucking companies; trucks are often old and roads poorly maintained; excessive regulation and stubborn corruption also suffocate the growth of a more modern logistics industry.

FOR ALL THE OPTIMISM ABOUT THE RISE OF THE EAST'S MIDDLE CLASSES, too little attention is paid to the risks of stagnation following economic or political crises. The slowing in China's economic growth during 2013 was indeed a warning shot that not even the region's largest economy is immune to risks.

No country better understands the risks than Thailand. It was here that Asia's financial crisis began in 1997 as a result of the country's worsening economic imbalances. The Thai stock market collapsed and lost 70 percent of its value over two years, and the Thai baht almost halved in value. Property prices collapsed, and Bangkok was littered with the skeletons of unfinished buildings for years. Layoffs surged, especially in finance and property, and incomes were slashed among those lucky enough to keep their jobs. There were only limited economic data at the time to track the depth of the crisis, but the middle class was eviscerated, rolling back the gains of a decade.

Even the super-rich were short of cash. Recognizing an opportunity, Wasant Pothipimpanon set up the iconic "Market of the Formerly Rich" in 1997 in the wealthy downtown district of Thonglor. The fabulously titled bazaar operated out of Wasant's Mercedes-Benz dealership and attracted wealthy households looking to raise some cash in tough times. "My clients had a lot of assets. The problem was they didn't have cash. And so they had to try to sell things to raise money," Wasant said. What type of things? "Oh, diamonds, jewelery, and cars. One of my clients had over 200 Mercedes-Benz cars." I ask him what the biggest item ever sold at the market was. "A 12-seater airplane," Wasant replies.[19]

I visited the dealership during a sticky summer in 2013. Wasant had briefly reopened his "Market of the Formerly Rich" in 2009 during the global financial crisis, but soon shut it down again for lack of demand. "What crisis?" he replied repeatedly to my questions. "Maybe it was a crisis for the rest of the world, but we didn't feel anything."

Thailand has certainly bounced back since 1997. But during those dark years it felt as if the country might never recover. Even if the full economic data aren't available to tell the story, there are plenty of middle-class families who can. Wasant might have been dealing with the super-rich at the time, but he was one such witness to the effects of the crisis on the ordinary middle class. "So many people lost their jobs," says Wasant. "Some worked for family companies. Some for international companies. Many were originally from outside of Bangkok and so had to return home once they lost their jobs."

And then he delivers the punch line: "These former white-collar workers had to work on the family farm in order to eat." Indeed, stories of salaried employees returning to their family's upcountry farms were not uncommon during Thailand's financial crisis. At the end of the day, we all have to eat.

Fortunately, the country has since recovered and Wasant's Mercedes-Benz dealership is surrounded by fancy bars and restaurants more suited to London or New York. For some of those laid off during 1997, the crisis was even a blessing as it prompted them to start a more entrepreneurial career. "I have white-collar friends who got their start because of the crisis. They were once salaried employ-ees living on bank credit or OPM (other people's money). But the crisis made them stand on their own feet and they set up a business. They say the crisis was the best thing that ever happened to them," laughs Wasant.

It might seem that the events of 1997 are unlikely to be repeated given how far the region has developed since then. During the worst of the crisis, Thailand's economy contracted 17 percent from peak to trough.[20] By contrast, during the recent global crisis, the American economy contracted just 5 percent.

And yet there are still reasons to worry about Asia's growth trajec-tory. Debt levels have risen steadily across the region, with corporate, household, and government debt expanding especially fast. The latter isn't terribly critical if the money is pumped into better infrastructure, but it also risks a growth slowdown if the government starts to tighten its belt. Corporate debt has also risen sharply in the past few years, and inevitable policy tightening by the US Federal Reserve, as the central bank ends its policy of quantitative easing, will also see capital leave the region, providing a further drag on growth.

But growth doesn't have to collapse for consumers to stop spend-ing. Inflation risks, for instance, were a major challenge for Chinese consumers during 2008 as food and housing prices soared, leaving households with less money to spend each month on discretionary items. Indeed, inflation averaged 4 percent across the region in the period from 2010 to 2012, as compared to a modestly lower 3.5 percent between 2005 and 2006, prior to the global financial crisis. Incomes are rising in many cases but do not always match the general rise in housing prices and food costs.

In Hong Kong, wages for semiskilled workers, earning between US$10,000 and US$20,000 per year, have only just kept pace with inflation since 2005, meaning no change in their purchasing power even as the dollar value of Hong Kong's economy expanded by nearly a third during the period. Moreover, workers in the manufacturing and transport sectors have seen their purchasing power fall as wages have stagnated in the face of stiff competition from China.[21] Much of that is the result of spiraling food prices, with food costs accounting for 30 percent of spending by a typical Hong Kong working-class family, as against just 20 percent for wealthier families.

Working-class families might not be big spenders, but they do have discretionary income to spend on goods and services and are therefore a target for local and foreign firms. They are also at risk of slipping back into poverty should food and energy prices rise at an even faster rate in the coming years.

THE RISE OF THE EAST'S CONSUMERS IS A POWERFUL STORY, BUT IT'S ALSO A very different challenge for the foreign companies that cut their teeth selling to Western consumers for the past 50 years. The best firms are already adapting, whereas those arriving late to the region are likely to find it exceptionally tough.

Much of the debate has so far focused on the cultural differences between markets. That's certainly critical. Take the researchers at Hong Kong's Polytechnic University, a short drive from my office in Central, where a team led by Roger Ball is measuring the head sizes of 2,000 Chinese people as part of the Size China project. Because most caps and helmets are designed to fit Western-shaped heads, they are uncomfortable when worn by many Asians. It's a simple yet overlooked point. The head-shape models that fill Bell's office are intended to correct this and produce a bump in Asian sales.

But the story is far bigger than this. The rise of Asia's consumers will both excite and disappoint as companies discover the challenges of selling to the region's shoppers. Trying to push into second- and third-tier cities will force foreign companies to invest in larger operations, even as they try to sell to more localized consumers. That's a risky bet for many. Tying up with local partners is a logical alternative, as a partner might better understand local tastes and have stronger distribution and marketing networks or critical relationships with local businessmen and officials. But it's also a decision that comes with its own set of opportunities and challenges.

The speed of change in the market will also leave many scrambling. Take China's wine market. In 2005, the country was importing just $75 million of wine annually. The figure had tripled to over $250 million by 2007.[22] How should a company position itself for such a sudden change in demand? Some firms will choose to invest speculatively in the hope that at least some of their bets will pay off. But that's always a challenge for publicly listed firms to explain to shareholders. Others will take the safer route of waiting for the change to happen but will subsequently fall behind the curve.

The potential fall in demand is equally important. Higher living costs are already eating into the budgets of many Hong Kong households, but this is also true in Indonesia, where rising food and fuel prices are a threat to the recent consumer boom. That may not be enough to prevent the 20- or 30-year surge in demand that Hartono Jap speaks of, but it may cause a dip in demand for premium beer and shampoo, for instance, as consumers opt to trade down as their purchasing power falls. Being in a position to respond to that sudden shift in consumer preferences is critical in the East.

Most explosive, though, is the combination of the East's dispersed populations, the high number of smart devices per person, and the strength of the region's e-commerce players. The high rate of smartphone penetration in the East is owed partly to the fact that many of the region's developing countries skipped a generation and invested heavily in mobile technologies rather than landlines. Might the same countries skip a generation when it comes to the way they buy? Why spend money on building fancy shopping malls or retail outlets when consumers are more likely to buy online?

In the West, malls and retail outlets are legacy assets. In the East, many are yet to be built and, indeed, may never be built. However, that still means that more will need to be spent on the region's infrastructure because shoppers will expect to wait days, not weeks, to receive their goods. China has succeeded in this by building a road infrastructure that allows for express delivery, similar to the region's more developed countries such as Hong Kong and the UAE. But India and Indonesia are two of the region's giants where improvements in logistics must be made.

2

THE END OF "MADE IN CHINA"?

MAJOR CHANGES AHEAD FOR MANUFACTURING

I T WAS CLEAR THAT THE HAI XING APPAREL COMPANY HAD A PROBLEM. The manufacturer in the southern Chinese city of Dongguan was part of a sprawling mass of industrial parks and factories that had thrived on its ability to attract cheap labor. It is a common practice in the city to advertise job postings on factory gates or walls, thus allowing migrant workers to walk or pedal their bikes from factory to factory looking for jobs. In the spring of 2012, I was standing outside the company's main gates reading a sandwich board advertising the positions on offer. A decade ago it was enough to advertise the available jobs and wage range in order to attract employees. But not anymore.

Hai Xing Apparel was offering *"annual leave, holiday leave, marriage leave, and maternity leave."* But it didn't stop there. The billboard also flagged "a starting bonus, a bonus for workers who return after the Chinese New Year, and a bonus for those who recommend new workers." It then went on to list all the amenities the factory offered to its workers, from ping pong tables to karaoke rooms.

Whether the factory filled the positions, I don't know. But while reading the sign, I watched three young workers exit the building, mobile phones in hand, their hair dyed and cut in a style that would suit the American pop star Justin Bieber, and wearing fashionable clothes that would look more appropriate in one of the nightclubs in Hong Kong's Mongkok district. These weren't the young migrant workers who drove China's export miracle in the 1990s, or even in the early 2000s, hungry to create a better life—these young workers already had a better life. Jobs weren't hard to find and smartphones offered cheap entertainment. So, what next?

Over the past 20 years, China has emerged as the world's manufacturing heartland. In some instances, Chinese manufacturers simply offered cheaper prices than did their foreign competitors. In others, Asian, American, and European firms boxed up their factories and moved to China. But the result was the same as China emerged as the world's largest producer of a range of goods—from toys to clothing to consumer electronics—finally overtaking Japan, the United States, and Germany to rank as the world's largest exporter, shipping over $2,000 billion, or 11 percent of the world's total in 2012.

For 20 years it was a relatively straightforward proposition: produce cheap in China and sell to the rest of the world. No other country had quite the same impact on the global supply chain. But then an earthquake struck China's manufacturing base.

The southern Pearl River Delta was ground zero. In 2005, the region's factories suddenly struggled to employ enough labor. It was a seismic shock for a supply chain that had thrived by employing cheap migrant workers from neighboring provinces. The Pearl River Delta itself covers an area similar to that of Denmark or the Netherlands. But it taps into a vast 300-million-person labor pool from surrounding provinces to assemble toys, construct buildings, or wait tables. Each year, some 10 million migrant workers are estimated to return home by train or bus during the Lunar New Year.[1]

But by 2013, the provincial government's labor department claimed that the Pearl River Delta and its factory cities were short over one million workers, a figure large enough to cut the US employment rate by nearly 0.6 of a percentage point.

Similar shortages emerged around the same time in other factory hubs along the eastern seaboard provinces—factories in Fujian, Zhejiang, Jiangsu, and Shandong all reported problems attracting enough labor. The problems eased during the global financial crisis as the country's exports collapsed. But they soon re-emerged as export growth resumed and as Beijing spent billions in the interior provinces building bridges, roads, and high-speed rail projects to prop up growth. The injection of cash created jobs for migrant workers who no longer felt compelled to make the trek eastward.

And it wasn't just the manufacturing base. The services sector was feeling the same pinch as companies across the country scrambled for the type of young, semiskilled workers that are a staple of China's labor-intensive export factories.

"It used to be that the hotel industry could offer great benefits," said Deng Yuanming, General Manager of the Jianguo Hotel in Beijing, one of the city's first international hotels. "But now everyone is offering a better package, whether they are a hotel or a factory." When we spoke in the summer of 2011, Deng put some of the blame on the interior provinces. "Beijing is an expensive place to live and the opportunities at home are growing, especially since the government has spent so much money in the interior provinces. Why not work at a local hotel nearer to your family and where living costs are much less?"[2]

Thirty years ago, Beijing's policy planners decided to limit the number of children the average family could have to just one. It was a time when the Chinese were clothed in the same green caps and Mao suits; little did those planners know that their decision would squeeze the country's industrialization three decades later. The number of births was already falling in the late 1970s, but it subsequently collapsed with the result that the country's youth population—those 15- to 30-year-olds who make up much of the export sector's migrant workforce—was forecast to decline by around 85 million people between 2010 and 2030.[3]

The data offer a compelling picture of the change. As part of my consulting work I had crunched trade customs data for over 1,200 export products; the results showed that Cambodia, Indonesia, and Vietnam were all enjoying stronger export growth relative to China in many low-end apparel and electronic products. Take knitted apparel as an example (and by knitted, I mean garments that can be pulled apart by pulling a single thread). The three countries have watched their shipments of knitted apparel grow faster than have China's own shipments of the same goods. Indeed, Cambodia and Vietnam recorded growth rates twice those of their larger northern neighbor.

Dig deeper into the details, and the gains are often concentrated in specific product segments: Cambodia has enjoyed large increases in its exports of footwear with plastic soles; Indonesia has benefited from strength in shipments of knitted sweaters and pullovers; Vietnam has enjoyed a jump in shipments of female non-knitted suits.

Demographics explain a good part of their success. The average Chinese working in a coastal export factory is 35 years old and earns around $300 a month. By contrast, the average Vietnamese is younger and cheaper at 29 years old and around $120 a month. It's a big difference and one that has attracted considerable investment into the country's export sector. The differences are starker when looking at China's even younger and cheaper competitors: the average Bangladeshi and Cambodian, for instance, is 24 years old and is paid around $80.[4]

The result is that China's once supercompetitive export sector is no longer looking so competitive. Manufacturers and sourcing companies are in turn looking to younger and cheaper Southeast Asia as an alternative. Even then, labor supply and price is just one part of the industry's growing complexities.

The offices of Marks & Spencer are in Hong Kong's Ocean Centre building, a short walk from Victoria Harbour and the neon-lit shops along bustling Nathan Road. The district is the first stop for tourists in the city. It is also the location of many of the world's big retail companies and sourcing companies, from global sportswear giants to Japanese toy makers—the district provides easy access to southern China's export factories by either ferry or train. It is here that decisions are made that can shift jobs around the world as sourcing companies switch buying from one country to another.

Richard Thomas is Head of Sourcing for the Far East Region at Marks & Spencer, the British multinational retailer. He has visited thousands of factories during the past 20 years and can recall almost every one. "I take pictures," he says. "It's the faces of the workers and factory managers that remind me of each place."

Thomas emphasizes that cost only partly explains the changes in the industry. "Sure, it plays a role. But it's also about balancing your portfolio. You need to source in countries with duty-free access to Europe or even local markets here in the region. You need to de-risk from countries with labor shortages. You need to dual-source some products," he says. "It's all these pressures that force change and so while we source one-third of our goods from China, we've also gone into Vietnam, Cambodia, and Bangladesh, and we're looking at new opportunities in Myanmar and Pakistan."

Factory migration also has its limits. "We are also increasingly focused on efficiencies in the markets we are already in," he emphasizes. "It is critical we maintain leading standards of ethics and quality. We are absolutely committed to the company's sustainability program, *Plan A*, especially when entering new markets."[5]

It's partly because of these pressures that the changes in the industry are unlike those that took place during previous decades when clothing factories in Korea and Taiwan or Mexico and Honduras all closed or relocated to China as global buyers responded to rising wages by searching for the next low-cost producer. For a start, the biggest retailers and sourcing companies already have a strong presence in multiple countries. But the focus on ethical and sustainable supply chains is understandably far greater than it was decades ago as foreign companies align themselves with new standards.

There is also one more major factor. "Tell them you've found the next China. That will get everyone's attention," whispered one of the organizers of a major sourcing conference in Hong Kong in 2011 as he guided me to the stage where I was about to deliver a presentation on changes in the region's manufacturing. It was friendly advice. The problem is that there *isn't* another China. This time, it really *is* different as the manufacturing and sourcing industry runs up against the end of the road. It is not an end to outsourcing itself, but rather a change in the way the industry has sourced over the past 50 years.

What really makes things different is China's size: the country is too big to replace. Consider Cambodia, a low-cost competitor and a country with a GDP of $14 billion. That makes it about the same size as a small suburb of Guangzhou, the capital of China's Guangdong province. In fact, China's monthly textile exports are larger than

Cambodia's annual GDP. To be fair, Cambodia is one of Southeast Asia's smaller countries. But Vietnam is one of the largest with a population of 88 million, and yet that is still smaller than Guangdong's 106 million people—before counting the province's undocumented migrant workers.

And even if Cambodia and Vietnam had the infrastructure to absorb China's low-end export processing industry (which they don't), such a shift would result in massive inflationary pressures as factories bid up costs for labor, raw materials, and logistics, not to mention the impact on property prices.

The result is that China retains the large share of the region's export manufacturing. It also still produces much of the materials and component parts that are used by factories around the region in their own export manufacturing. "I still expect China to be a major source of raw materials, yarns, fabrics, trims, and components for the region," says Marks & Spencer's Thomas. "We were sourcing fabrics from China more than 20 years ago, and we're still sourcing from the country today. China will be a major force for a long time to come—certainly well after I've retired from the industry."

The data confirm that complexity. Vietnam's imports from China of buttons, zippers, and non-adhesive labels, for instance, have soared from $17 million in 2005 to $79 million in 2012, illustrating the increasing interdependence of the region's supply chains as China spins off part of its production to neighboring countries.[6] And that's only for clothing. The average electronics product, by contrast, has significantly more component parts, meaning Southeast Asia's low-cost export manufacturers are even more reliant on imports not only from China, but also from the rest of North Asia.

A 30-minute drive outside the northern Vietnamese city of Hanoi, Samsung's giant factory is evidence of the growing complexity in the region's electronics supply chain. It is the Korean electronic company's largest mobile factory worldwide, employing some 24,000 people and producing mobile phones, refrigerators, vacuum cleaners, and other household goods. However, most of the component parts used in production are imported from Korea and other neighboring countries rather than being produced in Vietnam.

Hoang Anh Dung is Hanoi Manager for MACS Shipping and is responsible for shipping some of those component parts. Dung works for a state company, but he is an old-school entrepreneur and spends long evenings with his Korean clients, drinking to build relationships. To make up for that he bikes around Hanoi's beautiful West Lake at 6:00 a.m. every morning, before the city's raucous traffic begins. Dung provides logistics services for Samsung as well as for Nike and Orion, the Korean confectionery manufacturer, and I joined one of his weekly trips between his Hanoi office and the company's facilities at the Hai Phong port.

"We still import most of the component parts by sea-freight. It takes 21 days by road from Nanjing, but only seven days by sea," he says. It's a massive operation. "There are 1,000 containers arriving and departing each day from the factory. There are three teams working 24 hours just to process the factory's customs declarations."[7]

We drive in his car around the enormous plant. It takes a good ten minutes to pass by a long chain of complexes, each several stories high and housing dozens of production lines. "Most of the workers live in nearby areas, rather than dormitories, and are shipped in each day on 200 buses," he adds. In China, by contrast, workers arrive from across the country because coastal cities and provinces don't have sufficient labor supply to match demand. In fact, the factory itself lies in relatively open space rather than being surrounded by other factories, which is a more common sight in China.

We continue on to Hai Phong port, where the government, having started construction on a second port, has since opted to build a third that involves a huge new bridge across a river inlet. For now, there is a newly laid four-lane highway leading up the inlet, but no bridge as of yet. It is an ambitious plan that has many of Hai Phong's port operators scratching their heads. Vietnamese state planners certainly don't have the same track record as their Chinese colleagues. But given the growing volume of goods shipped to and from the country, you can certainly see why they are optimistic.

SOURCING COMPANIES INCREASINGLY TALK OF A "CHINA + 1" STRATEGY TO explain the dramatic changes. This means sourcing from China and at least one other country, but usually from multiple other countries. The change is evident in how China and Southeast Asia's share of American apparel and textile imports has risen from 19 percent in 2000 to 63 percent in 2011, with both China and Southeast Asia increasing their shares during the period.[8] The implication is that the developed world continues to be held hostage to the region's manufacturing. However, that only tells part of the story, as there are other changes at work.

The first is that the region is no longer simply exporting to households in America or Europe. In the winter of 2011, my family ordered some children's clothes from the Gap using its online store. Not a single item was produced in China, but rather in Indonesia, Vietnam, Bangladesh, and Pakistan. No surprise there. However, there was one important difference: we had placed the order not with the company's store in London, but rather with the company's new superstore in Shanghai. These low-cost Asian producers were selling not only to Americans and Europeans, but also to the increasingly affluent Chinese.

Asia is no longer just a cheap place to produce goods. It is also a place to sell goods. American and European shoppers still spend more on an individual basis, but it is the number of shoppers that matters for more affordable goods, such as clothing, and Asia has more shoppers than all of the developed world combined.

Ironically, it is the region's higher wages that are spurring that demand. Wages are rising not only in China, but also in the rest of the region. Indonesia hiked its minimum wage by around 20 percent in 2013, helped by the fact that manufacturing wages were still at least one-third lower than Chinese wages.[9] The Philippines, Thailand, and Vietnam have all raised their minimum wages repeatedly in recent years. Even Malaysia introduced a minimum wage for the first time in its history. The result was extra cash in the pockets of consumers to spend on goods usually produced at home or in a nearby country.

However, that creates a dilemma for factories faced with rising wages, especially factories in China. You could leave China for Bangladesh or Vietnam, where labor costs are cheaper. But why would you leave your fastest-growing market? Why leave China if you are increasingly selling to Chinese shoppers?

Many Chinese factories do indeed prefer to sell locally, says Professor Neale O'Connor, who has just completed a landmark study of over 1,000 Chinese suppliers. A longtime Hong Kong resident who is currently teaching at the National University of Singapore's business school, O'Connor toured trade shows and factory floors for over two years, interviewing factory owners. I am a big fan of this type of research in an era when "Googling" is an easy option, and I periodically caught up with O'Connor to check his results as new interviews were processed. In the autumn of 2013, we met for lunch in Hong Kong's Lan Kwai Fong district, a short walk from my office.

"There is a preference to sell to local buyers where there is a profitable opportunity. Language is of course important. But there are a number of other incentives. You are invoicing in the same currency, so there's no loss on the currency conversion. There's also less emphasis on the strict contract terms and conditions that foreign buyers will usually impose," says O'Connor. He then adds, "But money is ultimately the big driver and the domestic market is growing rapidly. I met one cashmere factory owner during my visits who claimed to be selling its products locally for four times what they were selling them abroad."[10]

The converts are not all local either. Gideon Milstein, owner of CBL Group, a contract manufacturer, is one such example. I visited Milstein's factory in Panyu in southern Guangzhou in the spring of 2012. The firm owns a design house in Australia and manufactures mainly OEM for clients selling in America and Europe, producing a range of goods including seats for New York City's Metropolitan Transportation Authority. When we spoke, however, Milstein was also developing a range of hospital beds for emerging markets, utilizing the firm's ability to design to Western safety standards, as well as to produce in a lean manufacturing environment.

"I'm looking at various emerging markets, where there is real demand for good quality, but highly cost-effective beds. Hospital beds aren't straightforward and we have designed products that incorporate Western safety standards and quality at a price that still needs to stack up against local products that might ignore these protocols," he said.

But 12 months later Milstein was selling mainly to China. "For the right products, margins are higher than they are for export in spite of the long distribution chains," he said in an email exchange. "We're making good headway by working in relatively niche, more difficult products. But even niche items in China have decent volumes due to the sheer size of the market. The lower end, basic bed market is very fragmented with no big players and thousands of cottage industry producers using their 'guanxi' [relationships] to gain business in their locality, which is why we design and make the products they can't."[11]

The result is that the largest share of the world's consumer-goods manufacturing is likely to remain stuck in Asia, but especially China, irrespective of the rise in production costs. There is simply no other region that has the capacity to supply Asia's hungry consumers: Sub-Saharan Africa is just one-third the size of Asia in terms of population; Latin America is smaller again; and eastern Europe barely registers. This is a big change from the 1990s when Asia's factories were tapping into vast pools of labor to supply relatively smaller populations in America and Europe.

THIS STORY OF RISING COSTS TWINNED WITH RISING DEMAND HAS A THIRD implication: many factories are considering whether it is time to produce their own brands rather than simply manufacture on behalf of others. It's not surprising, really. Factory owners can easily go online these days to calculate a retailer's markup on branded goods, which is significantly more than the factory-gate price. In the past, the idea of trying to produce branded goods for the American market was a step too far. But today, factory owners have the option of selling to the Chinese market, and that is compelling at a time of falling margins.

Ringo Mak is certainly a believer. We met during a conference panel session I was hosting in early 2013. The panel was aptly titled "Suppliers Today. Competitors Tomorrow." Mak, the President of Blue Box Toys, is one of those competitors, and I visited his office in Kowloon East a few months later to hear the company's story.

The best place to start is with Dedee Duck and friends, and Mak brought me to the company's showrooms to make the introductions. The baby toys are part of Blue Box's new portfolio, designed by the company's local designers and sold to toddlers around the world. Dedee is distinctive with an oversized head and a sweep of hair, or feather, sticking out from one side. His friend, Bebee Monkey, has the same stylish flourish. This feature is deliberate and part of Blue Box's strategy to sell branded toys, moving away from manufacturing toys for other retailers, and Dedee and Bebee's faces stare out from a range of pacifiers, rattles, and soft toys.[12]

It is a major change for this 60-year-old Hong Kong toy company. Peter Chan Pui, an immigrant from Guangdong province, established Blue Box in 1952, starting with a primitive plastic injection machine and producing homewares and simple toys. He called on the trading companies in Hong Kong's Central and Sheung Wan districts with bags of toy samples, and business soon grew. Chan was also unusual in that he enjoyed designing toys; as the company's chief designer, one of his earlier successes was a "drinks and wets" doll that could be fed water and peed when squeezed.[13]

For that reason, Blue Box has always stood out from its competitors. And while a large share of the company's business was contract manufacturing for the world's largest toy companies, Blue Box also developed new product concepts sold under the labels of those same companies. So it wasn't a surprise when the company decided to design, produce, and market its own brand. Perhaps it was inevitable that Chan's company would eventually pursue its own product lines. But Dedee Duck was also a response to the toy industry's falling margins as production costs rose and competition intensified.

For Chinese manufacturers, there are obvious attractions in evolving into brand owners. "We've had success, of course," Mak says. "But the change is also tough. It's like running two separate companies. One is run by engineers, the other by marketing and sales. They have two different sets of DNA."

Many Western companies would agree. The opportunity to have Chinese or other low-cost manufacturers produce under contract has allowed some of the world's biggest brands, from Victorinox to Samsonite, to largely exit from the manufacturing business and focus purely on marketing and distribution. After all, the money is in the brand itself, not the manufacturing process. Some brand owners are even calling on suppliers to conduct product research and development, thus allowing the company to further focus its efforts on marketing and distribution.

But it isn't possible to make the switch overnight. "We obviously can't produce goods that compete with the product lines of our existing clients. That's a tricky challenge. Ideally, we would stick to products where we have the most experience, but they are often the same products we are selling to clients," Mak says.

Yet, there is hope for Chinese manufacturers. While it is tough competing against clients in America and Europe, there are more opportunities at home and in the region's growing markets. The international toy companies and other retailers are certainly present, but not dominant. Chinese manufacturers also better understand local tastes and new fads, and so will be faster to respond to changing trends. And Chinese shoppers do have different tastes. "They are big fans of plastic toys with light and sound," says Mak. "You wouldn't try to sell wooden toys in China the same way you might in Europe."

We later walk through Blue Box's design studios, where desks and cubicle partitions are covered in half-made and finished toys. Four designers hold an impromptu meeting in one corner, staring intently at a small plastic doll. Most of the firm's designers were trained at the Hong Kong Polytechnic, a short walk from the company's offices in East Tsim Sha Tsui and near the cross-harbor tunnel connecting Hong Kong Island with the mainland. "Hong Kong designers are plugged into global trends. They can design for both markets," Mak says. "Still, mainland designers are improving fast."

I ask Mak if, given the option, he would forget about the manufacturing business. "Of course!" he replies. "Manufacturing is a real headache. Rising costs. Falling margins. Being a brand owner is the future."

"And if you wanted to succeed in ten years' time, which markets would you position for today?" I ask.

"China definitely," he replies, and then adds, "But also Southeast Asia. These are the growth markets."[14]

I LEFT AT 6:00 A.M. TO AVOID THE PROTESTS. IT WAS NOVEMBER 2012, AND Egypt's President Mohamed Morsi had granted himself immunity from the courts, an inflammatory decision that had angered his opponents. Massive protests were expected across the country, including in Cairo's Tahrir Square, a short walk from my hotel along the Nile. The protests had been building all morning and, so far at least, appeared far worse on CNN than they did in reality. But I had a meeting scheduled with SEZone, the operators of the country's new free zone located along the Suez Canal, and I didn't want to be late.

Business as usual? Not quite, but Egypt's political unrest hadn't resulted in the total collapse of the economy. The big international retail companies are still buying from Egypt in spite of the country's political challenges. Of course, by the summer of 2013, Egypt's political situation had worsened after the army opened fire on Muslim Brotherhood supporters outside Cairo's Rabaa Al-Adawiya mosque, killing more than 50. The army subsequently took a strong hand in ruling the country, and hopes for reconciliation rested on prospects for a return to a free electoral process and possible accommodation of the Brotherhood.

But an email sent to clients and investors by Oriental Weavers, one of the world's largest machine-woven rug and carpet manufacturers, neatly summed up the contradictory situation:

> Dear Sir or Madam: From your vantage point, it must be hard not to imagine that all of Egypt has downed its tools and headed to public squares across the nation to protest. Although the events of the past week and a half have been transformative for Egypt—and, indeed, may be far from over—it is still very much "business as usual" for Oriental Weavers as an Egypt-based multinational: our production facilities are fully operational in Egypt and around the world; all of our international clients' orders remain on schedule at all of our facilities; our logistics network remains undisturbed: Egypt's ports are open and maritime navigation has not been impeded.

Were they right? I checked in with Simon Kitchen, Strategist for EFG-Hermes, Egypt's largest investment bank, and a 12-year resident of Cairo. Kitchen was an old contact from previous visits to the city. "The curfew is still in place and that's caused some disruption to manufacturing and distribution, and also exports. But the regime has adopted a 'gloves-off' policy towards demonstrations, so we might see less disruption from strikes," he said.[15] Perhaps Oriental Weavers had a point, and certainly protests that look big on CNN are often limited to just a few city squares or districts.

Chances are that Egypt's situation will worsen before it gets better, and the risk of a civil war cannot be ruled out. However, the country's trade numbers also told a different story and gave me good reason to visit SEZone in the winter of 2012. I had crunched the numbers before my visit, and they showed that Egypt's exports of textile and knitted clothing products have continued to rise since 2005, dipping only modestly in 2008 during the global financial crisis. In fact, total textile and apparel exports were almost 20 percent higher in 2012 compared to five years earlier, in spite of the turbulence.

I later put the question to the heads of sourcing for a number of international retail companies back in Hong Kong. Some were planning to increase their orders from Egypt, while others were more cautious, but usually those looking at alternatives were responding to commercial pressures as much as political forces.

If countries such as Bangladesh and Vietnam are benefiting from China's rising prices, then why not Egypt or other countries around the world, such as Morocco, Turkey, Honduras, or Mexico? Wages in these countries are also relatively low, often lower than wages in China. Their apparel manufacturing sectors are also well established with close proximity to the big American and European markets. Even if political disruption does eventually hit output by Egypt's apparel and textile manufacturers such as Oriental Weavers, there are still some compelling alternatives outside of Asia.

Among the most important alternative is a growing preference to source nearer to the point of sale. In the case of European retailers, that means sourcing from Egyptian, Turkish, or other low-cost neighboring countries, rather than from East Asia. The strategy is called "nearsourcing," and it can cut total lead times by half, as goods spend around a week in transit on their way to Europe, rather than the six weeks when shipping from China and other East Asian countries. The same is true for American retailers looking to source from nearby countries such as Costa Rica.

That's important as, for all the talk about wage and raw material costs, one of the retail sector's biggest costs is marking down unsold goods in order to clear inventories. It's also important as today's consumers demand greater variety and the more regular introduction of new products. Shorter delivery times allow retailers to meet these twin challenges by placing smaller orders more frequently. No surprise that some of the world's biggest fast-fashion chains, such as Zara, the Spanish clothing and accessories multinational, rely heavily on near-sourcing.

This is the increasingly complex world that retailers and sourcing companies are operating in and, even as China's rising prices push some production into Southeast Asia, the attractions of near-sourcing strategies have many looking even further afield to countries such as Egypt and Turkey.

Mahmoud al Haddad would likely agree. He is the part owner of a factory in Yantai, a coastal city situated in China's Shandong province and a short flight from Beijing. His factory produces apple concentrate and pectin from locally sourced apples, exporting the product to Egypt and other countries in the Middle East where demand is strong. We met by chance on a flight from Dubai to Cairo (there's nothing like 30 inches of legroom and a long-haul flight to get people talking). Al Haddad was returning to Cairo from Beijing after a short two-day trip to China, and we struck up a conversation.

Most of his product was exported to the Middle East, especially Egypt where demand was strong post-revolution. "The foreigners have all left and there's no competition. I've had a record year," he said jokingly. "People still have to eat after all, no matter how bad it gets, and my products are basic staples."

Al Haddad is typical of the traders who are behind the Middle East's strong commercial ties with China. But his experience also illustrates the more complex reality of today's production chains. Al Haddad hadn't pulled out of Egypt entirely, and he still had a factory in the country, another in Dubai, and, of course, his factory in Yantai. He wasn't an apparel manufacturer, but he was well positioned to judge the relative competitiveness of low-cost manufacturing. Labor costs were one factor, domestic markets another. Near-sourcing was important. But there was one additional reason.

"For my product, Yantai is still the best option. Egypt just doesn't have the apple feedstock. In fact, it doesn't have much raw material apart from apples. But if you're talking about processing work, then it gets more interesting. We can mix, blend, assemble all sorts of goods in Egypt and then export them to Europe or Africa duty free," he tells me.[16]

Much like Cambodia's duty-free access to Europe, Egypt's duty-free access to Europe and Africa was seen by al Haddad as a competitive advantage. He wasn't the only one. The Chinese air-conditioning company Hisense built a factory in southern Cairo partly to service the local market. But in an interview with Chinese media, the company's manager, Ren Liren, was quoted as citing duty-free access to Africa as, again, a major reason to build factories in the country.[17] From clothing to apples to air conditioning, the attractions of proximity to market and duty-free access can be powerful drivers of trade flows, especially as China's costs rise.

To be sure, Egypt isn't a replacement for China, just as Cambodia and Vietnam are not a substitute for China. Productivity rates in China are far higher, as al Haddad argues. Add to that China's better quality ports, roads, electricity supply, and the country's vast economies of scale—all are reasons to stay in China.

But there is hope for Egypt and neighboring countries. And that's important at a time when jobs growth will be crucial to stabilizing social unrest. After all, China's annual exports to Europe are larger than Egypt's entire economy. And whereas China's youth population is forecast to fall by 44 million between 2010 and 2020, Egypt's is forecast to rise by only 600,000 as a result of falling birthrates over the previous decades.[18] So even a small relative shift in garment production from China to Egypt would not only provide jobs for new entrants to the jobs market, but also reduce the number of long-term unemployed.

THE IDEA THAT ASIA IS AN INCREASINGLY EXPENSIVE PLACE TO MANUFACTURE is not new. What is new is that China's sheer size means there is no simple substitute, and production will more likely disperse across the region, further complicating supply chains. Moreover, the fact that Asia itself is a major market means it is no longer a question of factories simply returning to America or Europe. To this end, the region is evolving much as America and Europe did, producing increasingly for the domestic market and developing its own brands as consumers look for more value-added products.

This means that much of the world's manufacturing capacity will remain trapped in Asia. Sure, there are other disruptive influences. Lower energy prices might draw some manufacturing back to America, especially in the chemical or other heavy-industry sectors. The commercialization of 3D printing and the ability to fabricate goods at home with a touch of a button might also reduce how much America buys from Asia. This would be welcome news for America, but the country is still likely to buy many of its low-end apparel and electronic goods from Asia, if only because the region will still account for the bulk of the world's production.

And how much does it matter for China or the rest of Asia? The region's dependence on its exports to the United States is falling steadily; combined exports to the world's largest economy were worth just 5 percent of GDP in 2012, against 9 percent a decade earlier, and this share will continue falling, as the region sells more at home than abroad. Indeed, the bigger threat for Chinese factories in the coming years is perhaps not whether American consumers start producing their own toys or household goods using 3D printers at home, but whether Chinese consumers do.

However, the underlying dynamics are good for the global economy. Manufacturing workers earn higher wages and so are able to spend more money on iPhones or movie tickets. Other low-cost countries, such as Egypt, also have a chance to reclaim manufacturing jobs, previously lost as a result of China's initial rise. Indeed, for all the talk about lost jobs in America and Europe, the rise of China has most impacted the emerging markets. In Pakistan, for example, the country's imports from China have risen to 23 percent of total imports and include a large number of apparel products, a traditional growth sector for Pakistan, which implies lost jobs and factory closures.[19]

The fact that China itself is buying more from the rest of the East is also a boon for other low-cost countries. In a sign of the change, foreign retailers are looking to source from countries with duty-free access not just to markets in America or Europe, but also to markets in China. The idea that China could yet create jobs in neighboring countries as a result of its buoyant consumer spending, is also supportive of the region's consumption. Indeed, China's rising costs have already removed the wage ceiling that kept wages low across the region, and governments across the East are happily increasing minimum wages as they worry less about losing competitiveness versus China.

The result is that anyone manufacturing or sourcing in the East will face an increasingly complex set of questions. Most importantly they will have to strike a balance between globalization and localization. The idea of cheap goods flowing from East to West is over. Increasingly, goods will flow East to East and West to West. Manufacturers in the East will also look more and more like those in the West as they attempt to build brands and sell to local buyers. To some extent, this resembles trade before globalization, when local manufacturers did sell primarily to local consumers. The difference is that globalization isn't leaving anytime soon; instead, the two trends are merging.

3

TAPPING INTO THE
MUSLIM MARKET

WHY A HALAL STRATEGY IS
CRITICAL FOR GROWTH

IN THE SPRING OF 2012, I WAS ENTERTAINING A SYRIAN FRIEND IN Hong Kong. We were in Central and wanted to eat halal food. I knew of restaurants on the Kowloon side where the Pakistani community is concentrated, but not on Hong Kong Island itself. We ended up eating at an Ebeneezer's kebab outlet in Lan Kwai Fong where a paper certificate from Hong Kong's Islamic Community Fund vouching for the restaurant's halal certification was displayed prominently in the window. It wasn't a fancy meal, but for Muslim visitors to a non-Muslim country, takeaway at the local kebab store or Indian restaurant is standard fare.

A year later, I downloaded Zabihah's mobile app. The app ranks over 15,000 halal restaurants worldwide, providing a location service for hungry tourists. I soon discovered 93 restaurants in Hong Kong, including a branch of Pret A Manger, the British sandwich chain, just below my office in the Central MTR Station and where I often eat lunch. Little did I know that I was eating halal chicken wraps.[1] There are over 1.3 million Muslim tourists who visit Hong Kong each year, many passing through Central Station, and I can imagine Pret A Manger does good business through its reference on Zabihah.

The app is one of a growing number targeting Muslims across the region as they eat, shop, or go on vacation and make informed choices about their halal options. Just as companies are looking to tap into the Chinese or Indian market, leading firms are targeting the Muslim consumer.

The East's Muslim population is like a spine running through the region. Take a look at any map: the region stretching from Cairo to Mumbai to Jakarta and finally to Beijing includes nearly 50 countries. Of these, 31 are majority Muslim countries and a further seven, such as India, Singapore, and even China, have large Muslim minorities. Together, the region's Muslim population totals 1.1 billion and accounts for a huge 88 percent of the world's Muslims.[2] No other ethnicity or religious group—whether Chinese or Indian, Buddhist or Hindu—has the same spread across the East.

The East is the heart of the Muslim world, and the Muslim world lies at the heart of the East; to ignore the Muslim world's role in the East's rise would be to overlook one of the region's more important commercial dynamics.

For a start, there is a similarity between the East's Muslim markets. Majority Muslim countries tend to be young, with an average age of 25 years, as against an average age of 30 years for the East's non-Muslim markets.[3] This is not necessarily true for all Muslim countries—Kuwait and Turkey, for instance, are older than average—but youth is nevertheless a feature of Muslim countries, and it is perhaps no surprise that the Arab revolutions have occurred at a time when many Muslim countries have seen a jump in their youth populations.

The East's Muslim economies are also booming, growing an average 6 percent since 2008, similar to the world's other fast-growing emerging markets, including many East Asian economies.[4] It is a strong improvement on the previous two decades when growth averaged a lower 4 percent and tended to fluctuate more wildly, and is especially impressive when compared to Europe and the United States, where growth averaged between zero and one percent during the same period and remains weak as a result of earlier financial excesses.

Of course, it helps that the East's Muslim economies are sitting on much of the world's oil. Together, they account for 35 percent of the world's oil production and an even larger 49 percent of the world's oil reserves.[5] Saudi Arabia, Iran, Iraq, and Kuwait account for the largest share, but oil is also found in Algeria, Kazakhstan, Malaysia, and Indonesia, to name just a few countries. Islam might have arrived centuries before the discovery of oil, but through good fortune, the religion spread through countries where oil is easy to extract.

These similarities are important as Islam shapes commercial opportunities. Take the Christian holiday Christmas as an example: in the United States, over 10 percent of retail consumer goods are sold in the final month of the year. The Muslim festivals have a similar effect on sales, especially during the monthlong Ramadan fast: food consumption rises steeply as families and friends get together after sunset, and even during the early hours of the morning, to break their daily fast; advertisers flock to the popular Ramadan television soap operas shown during the month; even e-commerce sales enjoy a bump from shoppers up at odd hours.

Yusuf Hatia understands the importance of those figures. He is Managing Director for FleishmanHillard, a global communications company, and oversees the firm's India operations. However, I am speaking with Hatia because he is also head of the firm's recently established Majlis, a specialty service created to assist companies in building their reputation with the Muslim community. I first met Hatia in the autumn of 2011 at the Arab-China Trade Forum in China's western Ningxia province. But this time we are speaking in the lobby of the Grand Hyatt in Mumbai, just opposite his office.

"Multinationals are looking for the next big thing. They may have a China strategy, an India strategy, and an Africa strategy. But what's next?" he says. "There simply isn't another China, India, or Africa out there. That's why they are turning to the Muslim consumer—it is large, lucrative, and underserved."[6]

I dug out the data after speaking with Hatia to check his point. The East's Muslim population totals 1.1 billion, or larger than that of Sub-Saharan Africa. It is also expected to rise to near 1.3 billion by 2025, based on United Nations demographic projections, and with an average age of 30, will still be ten years younger than the average Chinese.[7] What is especially exciting about these consumers is that many are living in newly emerged countries, such as Indonesia, and so are unbanked and unbranded, unlike consumers in China, where markets have matured fast and consumers are spoilt for choice.

Multinationals and fleet-footed midsized companies are responding. "It's the West that is ironically driving much of the debate around halal. I spend as much time being asked to pitch to senior executives in New York and London on halal consumer relations as I do here in the region. They understand the scale of the opportunity," Hatia says.

Nestlé, the Swiss food and beverage multinational, is one of the global leaders in the development of halal products. Since the 1980s, the company has offered halal versions of its most famous brands, including KitKat and Smarties confectionery, Maggi soups, Milo malted drinks, and Nescafé coffee. Many of the company's 85 halal-certified factories are in Indonesia, Malaysia, the Middle East, and Turkey. But at least 20 of the firm's European production lines are also halal certified, underscoring the strength of demand in those markets.[8]

Unilever is a more recent arrival in the halal market. But the Anglo-Dutch consumer goods company sells some of the world's best-known soap and cosmetic brands, such as Dove soap and Sunsilk shampoo. Traditionally, animal fats, including pork fat, are among the main ingredients in any soap or cosmetic product. Islamic countries, such as Indonesia and Pakistan, are some of Unilever's largest markets, so developing halal-certified products is critical to the company's continued growth in the emerging world.

Food is just one segment of a halal market that includes finance, fashion, and pharmaceuticals among a range of goods and services commonly consumed across the Muslim world. Some products result from a few laws that apply to all Muslims, no matter where they live, such as *zakat* and halal food. Other products are associated with the holy month of Ramadan, such as pilgrims catching flights during the Eid or families buying dates at the local supermarket. These so-called market verticals create opportunities to benefit from scale and efficiency by tapping into the global Muslim market.

YET, THE IDEA OF A "HALAL" PRODUCT ALSO OVERSIMPLIFIES THE OPPORTUNITY. Targeting a religious community living across multiple countries and cultures makes the Muslim consumer harder to define than the

Chinese, Indian, or African consumer, and it isn't enough to simply produce a parallel range of halal products and hope they sell.

"You can't treat Muslims as a homogenous group," warns Hatia. "What binds them together is a common set of rules. But these rules can differ between countries and cultures. Muslims live in every country in the world, represent every race, and come from every social and economic stratum. And although they share the common thread of their beliefs, they have their own cultural, regional, or local nuances, preferences, and practices. The diversity of the Muslim consumer can prove to be a challenge to those who view markets as geographies and for whom the concept of an Islamic consciousness operating across market frontiers is alien."

Take Nestlé's Taste of Home product range, which includes the halal-certified Maggi *chorba* soup. The soup is suitable for all Muslim consumers, but it is popularly prepared by Moroccan households during the holy month of Ramadan and so sells best in North Africa as well as in Europe, where there is a large North African population. The product might be halal, but that doesn't mean it will sell well among the East's 1.1 billion Muslim consumers, especially in Southeast Asia. By contrast, Nestlé's Taste of Asia *rogan josh* paste, a popular Indian ingredient, has a more definable market.

There is also the challenge of selling products in non-Muslim countries. Some seven countries in the East have large minority Muslim populations, of which India's Muslim community is the largest at around 170 million people. Hatia offers an illustration of the risks of pitching to the Indian Muslim consumer: "Turkey is no problem. It's a majority Muslim country. But India is more challenging. Indian companies don't advertise their products as suitable for Hindus, so they worry what their core consumer base might think if they advertise products as suitable for Muslims."

For some foreign companies, such fears might include alienating core consumers back in the West. Dig around the websites of many big multinationals, and few refer specifically to their halal products, even if such products are available. The experience of KFC, the American fast-food chain, is a good example of how consumers in the West are sensitive to perceptions of "halal by stealth," as Hatia refers to it. When KFC removed bacon from the menu at 100 of the firm's 750 British stores in 2010, the result was a nasty consumer backlash, including negative press in the British tabloids.[9]

Producing a range of halal products isn't the only solution. Instead, it may be enough to simply tweak a marketing strategy for existing goods. "Nicorette is a good example," says Hatia. "They usually see strong sales during the New Year when sales jump as smokers promise to quit. But many Muslims quit temporarily during Ramadan, as smoking is prohibited by religious law during the fast. Smokers will go out and buy Nicorette patches to get through the month. It's a Ramadan sales bump, and Nicorette has a whole extra month to invest in sales, whereas they might have once only invested before New Year's."

Western Union is another example. "The company does good business transferring remittances and *zakat* payments for Muslim customers. So they set up Western Union–branded telescopes in mosques in India during the recent Ramadan holiday allowing Muslims to view the moon with the naked eye," says Hatia, referring to the practice whereby the arrival of the new moon signals the end of the religious holiday (and the fast). "Mosques aren't closed to promotion of halal products. Just look at Turkey, where most mosques will have restaurants, bookshops, and other facilities," he adds.

These complexities might encourage some to simply avoid the topic altogether. In the past, that might have worked, but not any longer.

"Companies must have a halal strategy or face ignoring what is likely to be a third of humanity. For example, if you're in the business of producing food and you don't have a halal strategy, you can't really consider yourself to be a global company," says Hatia.

"Muslim consumers are becoming more active. They are going online to discuss halal products. They are using mobile apps to identify what is and isn't halal. Most Muslims aren't represented in the mainstream media and so they are used to debating these issues only among family and friends. But that's all changed in the past decade and companies must be aware if their products are part of the discussion." One such community on Facebook has more than one million members and actively discusses brands such as Nestlé, Mars, and Unilever. Yet, the brands themselves do not appear engaged in the conversation.

It's not hard to find that debate online. Take a popular Muslim consumer group website in the United States where products are detailed by various product categories and brands. The site's members independently identify each product's ingredients: Vidal Sassoon shampoo? No guarantee it is pork free if other ingredients aren't available. Crest toothpaste? No animal-derived ingredients and no alcohol used in the flavor. Wrigley chewing gum? No animal-derived ingredients and no alcohol, but the possibility of cross-contamination from non-halal ingredients.

"MAKE SURE TO DRESS CASUALLY," WARNED ALWI AIDID. "IT'S VERY HUMID." He wasn't wrong: I started to sweat immediately after arriving at his warehouse in Singapore's northern suburbs where workers graded woodchips into large plastic bins. Aidid is a Singaporean national, but also a fifth-generation Hadrami from the Hadramout region in Yemen. His ancestors first migrated to Indonesia in the mid-1800s, and then to

Malaysia, before finally settling in Singapore, where Aidid was born. His late father built a flourishing business trading with Kuwait, Saudi Arabia, and other Gulf countries.

Aidid sold agarwood, or *oud*, a woodchip popular across the Middle East for its sweet smell. It is especially popular in the Gulf where a host might greet his guests at the door with chips of *oud* burning on coals in a silver censer. The wood is the result of infestation by weevil-like borers and is found mainly in wild forests in Indonesia, Malaysia, and other parts of Southeast Asia. *Oud* is popularly used by Muslims in the Middle East, but mainly for cultural reasons; it is also popular among the region's non-Muslim populations.

In fact, when I called Aidid several years later, it appeared that Chinese buyers were driving prices up. Many traditionally purchased the product for medicinal properties. But his new customers were buying it for other purposes; among these customers were the country's new rich, who were buying large, high-grade pieces of the wood for display in their grand mansions as status symbols. "Can you believe one buyer bought a high-grade piece weighing over five kilos for $2.5 million?" said Adid. "Crazy!" Nevertheless, it was still Muslim buyers that accounted for the larger share of the company's sales.[10]

Aidid's story illustrates how the strong ties between the Muslim world, after centuries of migration and trade, have resulted in many shared cultural habits or tastes; targeting the Muslim consumer may simply be an act of recognizing the community's cultural, rather than religious, similarities.

Bangkok's Bumrungrad Hospital has benefited by recognizing that distinction. In the summer of 2013, I was seated in front of one of their Arabic-speaking reception staff at the hospital's international counter. His Arabic was good. The same was true for the colleague sitting next to him who was walking a Middle Eastern client through the check-in procedures. That was impressive as both were Thai nationals. "Where did you study?" I asked. "Pakistan," he replied. "I'm a Muslim though, so I wanted to study classical Arabic." We chat briefly in Arabic before he attends to his next client, a patient from the Gulf.

Dr. Borihan has even better Arabic language skills, and for a good reason: he lived in Egypt for many years. "They think I'm an Arab," he says with a laugh when I ask how patients respond. But he then adds that most important is his ability to translate the cultural needs of his Middle Eastern patients to local staff.

Bumrungrad Hospital's major attraction is the quality of its medical staff. Many of Thailand's top doctors have studied and worked overseas, and most eventually return to the country with the ability to speak multiple languages. The hospital attracts the best of those returnees. In the early 2000s, the hospital received just 10,000 Middle Eastern patients a year, but the numbers subsequently soared as many patients found it harder to visit America and Europe after the September 11 attacks. The hospital also signed agreements with government agencies in Oman and the UAE. By 2012, the figure had jumped to 130,000 Middle Eastern residents out of a total of 520,000 international patients.

The results show. The hospital's lobby looks more like a five-star hotel in Dubai, full of men in white dishdashas and women wearing black abayas, much as they might in the Gulf, and looking comfortable as they mix freely with the Asian, American, and European patients. It's as if they had never left home.

"Our cultural sensitivity is also a key selling point," says Kenneth Mays, the hospital's marketing director and a longtime resident of Bangkok. He then offers an example: "The families of our Middle Eastern patients enjoyed congregating in some of the public areas of the hospital, chatting and drinking tea much as they might at home. That occasionally created tensions with other nationalities who felt the families had taken over the space. But that is how people from the Middle East relate. It's important to them. So we had to deal with it in a way that made everyone happy."[11]

Is Bumrungrad Hospital deliberately targeting a Muslim consumer, as Nestlé might with its halal-certified KitKat? Sure, the hospital provides an Imam during religious festivals, as well as halal food and a prayer room. But Dr. Borihan's sensitivity to the needs of Middle Eastern patients and the hospital's tolerance for Middle Eastern families congregating in waiting rooms is not a religious issue, even if those families are behaving in a way common among Muslim families from the Middle East. For Bumrungrad Hospital, the ability to appeal to Muslim patients means offering more than "halal" medical care.

COMPANIES SUCH AS NESTLÉ, WESTERN UNION, OR BUMRUNGRAD HOSPITAL provide insights into the complexities of selling to the Muslim world. But so do China and the Chinese Communist Party. In 2010, the western Chinese province of Ningxia, the historical home of China's minority Hui Muslim community, decided there was money to be made in Islamic tourism, Islamic food, and Islamic finance. The ruling Communist Party approved the province's intention, recognizing the opportunities to leverage the province's religious and cultural ties to the wider Muslim population in the East to the benefit of a relatively poor and landlocked population.

In the spring of 2012, I attended the China-Arab Trade Forum in Yinchuan, the capital of Ningxia province, to host a panel of Arab and Chinese guests. The forum is Ningxia's headline event and is intended to drive the province's Islamic-centered growth strategy. It was at the same forum where I had met FleishmanHillard's Yusuf Hatia a year earlier. Banners written in Arabic, Chinese, and English stretched across the freeway leading from the airport into town: *Welcome all to the China-Arab Trade Forum!* Even the street signs in the city's center had been updated so they read in both Chinese and Arabic.

Yinchuan's air is fresh and the sky blue, a remarkable sight in today's China. The city lies on the edge of China's western plains, and I am often tempted to hire a car and just keep driving northwest from the airport. The Hui Chinese, estimated at 10 million, have a similar wanderlust and are scattered across the country. Much like young workers from Anhui or Sichuan province, Ningxia's Muslim youth go to find jobs in the factories and restaurants along China's wealthier coast, especially Yiwu and Guangzhou, where they often work as translators, similar to the Muslim Thais working in Bumrungrad Hospital.

It is in Ningxia that China's Muslim past mixes with its present as Beijing's state planners experiment with the Muslim economy. Even as China faces unrest among the country's Muslim Uyghur population, the government sent the then Commerce Minister, Chen Deming, and other senior delegates to open a conference promoting Islamic trade and finance. Indeed, during this particular visit, I found myself in discussion with a senior member of the advisory board of China's State Administrator for Foreign Exchange, a body responsible for the country's 3 trillion dollars' worth of foreign reserves.

I would like to see the province succeed, not least because Ningxia's public and private sectors are working hard to meet their goals. Even while writing this chapter in the late summer of 2013, I received another email from the forum's business development team, diligently seeking feedback on their previous events. And yet, the city has its issues: limited manufacturing capacity, no direct international air links, and it is more than 600 miles from the nearest port. Visitors from North Africa were horribly jetlagged, having flown first to Dubai, then to Beijing, before finally arriving in Yinchuan.

By contrast, it is China's non-Muslim provinces, especially the coastal city of Yiwu in Zhejiang province, that are doing brisker trade with the Islamic world. The city receives some 200,000 Arabic traders each year who shop at the city's vast exhibition halls. Whereas Yinchuan is trying to tap into one of the Islamic world's "verticals," Yiwu is following a model similar to that of Bumrungrad Hospital. The city's biggest attraction is primarily the price and range of its consumer goods, ranging from toys to hardware, rather than its religious heritage. For a sole trader, it's possible to restock after just a few days of shopping.

Much like Bumrungrad's doctors, Yiwu's traders are also sympathetic to the needs of their customers: some products have universal appeal, such as a hammer; others have cultural appeal, such as an Egyptian festival lantern; and others have a specific religious attraction, such as a wall decoration with a Quranic inscription. The city has more than a dozen Arabic restaurants that serve halal food, but the restaurants compete with each other on the style of food they serve— from Egyptian to Syrian to Yemeni. Perhaps it is only the city's mosque that has strict religious appeal, as opposed to the other attractions of a commercial and cultural nature.

Yiwu's experience illustrates that it's not enough to be halal in the competition for Muslim consumers. The city has struck the right combination of price, range, and logistics, as well as making visitors from the mainly Muslim Middle East comfortable, from ensuring enough Arabic-speaking translators to permitting the city's Muslim community to fund an expansion of Yiwu's main mosque. More impressively, Yiwu achieves all this in a city where the Muslim community is a minority. But then perhaps Yiwu's traders are more focused on making "the next dollar" than they are worried about "halal by stealth."

IN THE SUMMER OF 2013, I WAS IN HONG KONG'S INTERNATIONAL AIRPORT waiting for my flight to Dubai when I noticed television monitors detailing a list of countries with travel warnings against them: Syria, Egypt, and Lebanon all made the "critical" list. Among those 16 countries that made the "cautionary" list, eight were, unfortunately, Muslim countries.

For all the optimism toward Muslim consumers, it would be equally wrong to ignore the challenges of social and political unrest in the Islamic world. Household finances in Egypt, for example, have taken a battering as a result of ongoing unrest and the collapse in tourism earnings that is impacting the ability of Egypt's Muslim consumers to spend. Much the same can be said for households in Libya or Tunisia. Were the unrest to spread further across the region, especially to the relatively wealthy Gulf countries, companies specifically targeting Muslim consumers might see a downturn in profits.

The story of Syria is particularly personal. It not only is one of my favorite countries but also featured heavily in my last book, *The New Silk Road*, as China had identified Syria as a stable hub for selling into the region's neighboring and less-settled countries, with the Adra Free Zone outside Damascus key to that strategy. And if Syria is central, then so is the story of my good friend Tayseer. I have known Tayseer for almost a decade. In fact, it was Tayseer who accompanied me when I visited the Adra Free Zone, an industrial park outside Damascus with a large Chinese presence, while researching my earlier book, as he had worked briefly in the zone as an accountant.

In the summer of 2011, I brought Tayseer to Hong Kong, where he lived for four weeks in a subdivided flat in Hong Kong's Sheung Wan district. The area is Hong Kong's original commercial district and was the first point of arrival for British merchants in the 1800s. It is also a sensory shock for the new arrival, as the streets are cluttered with competing neon signs hanging over the road and a jumble of small shops selling shark fins and Chinese medicines that produce a rich aroma. The flat was ideal for a short stay, and Tayseer settled in comfortably, ready to pick up his Chinese language studies with a local tutor.

But his plans didn't work out. Syria's conflict tragically worsened, and one of the region's once most stable countries saw fighting erupt in almost every city. By the winter of 2013, and after his return to Syria, Tayseer had left Damascus and settled in Istanbul, joining the 1.5 million other Syrians forced to flee their homes.

It is a sorry turn for a country that had long welcomed the region's other refugees. I recall an incident in the summer of 2010 at a small kebab shop in Damascus. While I was waiting, two Iraqi immigrants entered, an elderly mother wearing a black abaya, and her daughter. The daughter asked the shop owner's small boy to find a chair for her mother, and he scampered behind the counter, returning with a plastic chair and setting it down near a fan in the shop's corner. The mother sat down in relief, as the grill in the shop made the temperature ten degrees warmer than it was outside.

"There's so many of us Iraqis in Syria," she said, apologetically addressing the shop owner. "You must be tired of us by now."

"Of course not," the shopkeeper replied, brushing off her concerns. "Syria is open to all."

Iraqi refugees were only the latest arrivals in Syria's recent history. The country's problems are not unique in a region vulnerable to instability. Trying to zero in on a single reason for conflict is impossible—an authoritarian regime, youth unemployment, and income inequality all play a role and are issues that could affect any country in the region. Religious differences are more specific to the Muslim community, especially at a time of growing tensions between the Sunni and Shia communities, and such tensions may well shape the economic trajectory of the Muslim consumer.

There is also the possibility of tensions between the region's Muslim and non-Muslim countries impacting household wealth. Take the recent surge in violence between Myanmar's Buddhist majority and Muslim minority, or the simmering conflict in Thailand's southern provinces, where many of the country's nearly 4 million Muslims live. China's response to the 2009 clashes between the Uyghur minority and the Han majority in the western province of Xinjiang led to public outrage in Saudi Arabia and continues to threaten China's reputation in the kingdom, although it has yet to shake bilateral relations.[12]

Such volatility creates a unique challenge for companies targeting the Muslim consumer in the East. Household spending habits can change rapidly either as a result of conflict at home, or if households and governments have to provide financial support to large numbers of refugees from neighboring Muslim countries. Equally, worsening relations between Muslim and non-Muslim countries may make it problematic to publicly target Muslim consumers in non-Muslim countries and may leave companies wary of branding their products as halal outside of key Muslim markets.

It's no surprise then if many companies initially stick to a short list of countries, such as Indonesia and Malaysia, or the wealthier markets in the Gulf. The downside of such a strategy is that it excludes some two-thirds of the region's other Muslim consumers. The upside is that these countries are still relatively large markets in their own right, thus allowing companies to develop a product mix and marketing experience with which to later tap more challenging markets, much as foreign firms might tap China's larger coastal cities before venturing into the more challenging inland regions.

MUCH OF THIS BOOK FOCUSES ON OPPORTUNITIES IN THE EAST. HOWEVER, in the case of Muslim consumers, it is critical to recognize opportunities that transcend East and West. The importance of a common set of laws to the Islamic world means that the shopping habits of Muslim consumers in Jakarta or Riyadh, for instance, are often similar to those of a Muslim consumer in New York or London, and this provides a unique opportunity to cross-sell. The Zabihah mobile app, for instance, was created by Muslim entrepreneurs in Silicon Valley and is primarily used in America and Europe, but also increasingly in Asia and the Middle East.

This allows a company to hedge its exposure to unsettled markets in the East, such as Syria and Pakistan, or even India and Indonesia if economic conditions worsen, by also selling to the Muslim consumer in the West, such as in the United Kingdom, where the Muslim community is estimated at 2.7 million.[13] That is a smaller figure relative to many Islamic countries in the East, but the British Muslim community also has higher purchasing power owing to the fact that they live and work in a more developed country. Many are also looking for alternatives as a result of living in a non-Muslim country.

Of course, this doesn't overlook the challenges of selling products across multiple cultures: the market for a halal version of British staple products, such as Coleman's mustard or Branston pickle, is likely limited across the East. But it does create opportunities for other products, especially finance.

"Islamic finance is one of the more successful products sold across the Muslim world," says Omar Shaikh, the former London-based leader of Islamic financial services for Ernst & Young and Board Member of the Islamic Finance Council UK (UKIFC). "If you look at say car or housing financing products, there is a large degree of consistency between products. Globally, scholars claim there is 90 percent agreement on Islamic financing structures. This is partly because the scholars determining the legality of these products have a truly global footprint. Look at the makeup of Shariah Boards in Bahrain, the UK, or Malaysia, and you'll see a similar set of names."[14]

This global footprint means institutions such as Scottish Widows Investment Partnership, Standard Chartered Saadiq, and Bank of London and the Middle East can offer a consistency of shariah-compliant products across a wide range of markets, simultaneously targeting not only Muslim households in the East, but also those in America and Europe. The scale and connectivity can be a major commercial advantage. By contrast, a retail bank or fund manager has fewer ways to differentiate their product when targeting a Chinese or Indian household living in America or Europe.

Shaikh now shuttles between London, Asia, Africa, and the Middle East, advising companies and governments on Islamic finance. Together we collaborate through RHT Partners, a Dubai-based investment platform that focuses on cross-border opportunities, primarily in the East, and we periodically catch up in Dubai and London, allowing me to tap his views on opportunities in the West. "The UK Muslim consumer remains underserviced in the Islamic financial sector. There are no insurance or *takaful* providers and a limited retail banking offering. However, it's a new sector and continues to grow," he says.

That is one reason that Shaikh is in the process of examining an interfaith bank. "In the West, there is a unique opportunity to market Islamic finance on its ethical principles. The moral bankruptcy highlighted by the recent LIBOR scandals, miss-selling, and bonus debacle coupled with the systemic risks of the 'too big to fail' environment has resulted in many people in British society, regardless of faith, wanting to see a more socially responsible banking sector," he says. "At the UKIFC we've been holding a series of ethical finance roundtables and exploring the possibility of setting up a joint venture with the Church of England to create an interfaith bank based on the shared values."

The idea of an interfaith bank operating on shared values would certainly help to build scale, critical to any successful retail bank. Nor are the opportunities limited to banking. Saaf Pure Skincare, a British cosmetics company, produces its own range of skincare products that are certified halal, as well as organic and vegan. The company claims to receive over three-quarters of its orders from non-Muslims, having recognized the crossover between halal and other consumer concerns on a product's purity, with inquiries reportedly coming from Bangladesh, Canada, Australia, Belgium, and Malaysia.[15]

There are plenty of examples of cross-selling in the East itself, such as in Malaysia, where ethnic Chinese-Malays account for 40 percent of shariah-compliant investment product sales, or in China, where halal food products are viewed by some non-Muslims as safer than ordinary products. Indeed, given that Chinese consumers already associate halal with purity, Saaf Pure Skincare might profit from tapping into the growing numbers of Chinese shoppers visiting Hong Kong to buy natural-based cosmetics products that are hard to find back home. And if not a shop in Hong Kong, then why not turn to e-commerce?

Companies designing a halal strategy might set out to target the Muslim consumer, but that shouldn't limit a company's ambitions to only the Muslim consumer or only the East. The opportunities for cross-selling are significant, as Omar Shaikh, Saaf Pure Skincare, or Chinese halal food companies will argue.

INDEED, THE IDEA OF A HALAL PRODUCT IS TOO EASILY INTERPRETED AS targeting a large but niche market. Yet the lessons of Nicorette, Bumrungrad Hospital, Yiwu's exhibition halls, or Shaikh's interfaith bank argue in favor of staying flexible and looking for nontraditional opportunities even outside the halal market itself.

The challenge is finding the right people to identify and exploit the opportunities. "The creative industries struggle to attract Muslims, other than in countries like Indonesia and Malaysia," says FleishmanHillard's Yusuf Hatia, referring to the public relations and marketing industry. "You don't have to be Muslim to sell to Muslim consumers, but it helps. In the early 1990s, I remember being approached by a Malaysian firm called IslamIQ targeting middle-class Muslims in London. They had taken on a British PR company, but IslamIQ's CEO had to explain what shariah-compliant meant or the concept of non-interest based banking every time they met with the firm. She told me, 'It's a real difficulty.' They represent us, but they don't get our consumer."

The differences between cultures make the challenge even greater: a Saudi might have a good understanding of the Gulf market but might struggle to sell in Indonesia. The challenge for foreign companies is building a talent pool of experience that can be transferred between markets.

It may be that strategies are divided up between the regional offices and head office. Where a product is transferred across markets, such as Unilever's Dove Soap or Nestlé's KitKat, a company can more easily adopt a global strategy for selling that product to all Muslim markets; multinationals are best positioned in this instance. When the product is tailored to a specific culture, such as McDonald's Ayam Goreng chicken, the regional office is likely to take the lead, tapping into the country's local expertise; here, competition between multinationals and local firms will be more robust.

Developing online strategies is also critical as Muslim consumers are spread out across multiple countries and difficult to target through a single advertising campaign. The Muslim community is certainly switched on: over half of Malaysia's population has a Facebook account, as do one-third of Indonesians and one-fifth of Saudi Arabians. Online media also makes it easier to reach market subsegments, such as difficult-to-reach Muslim women and Muslims living in non-Muslim countries such as India, or even America and Europe, where Muslims receive only limited exposure in the traditional media.

Smaller foreign companies might consider the opportunity daunting. But selling to Muslim communities in America or Europe before selling in the East is an easier first step. Take Freemans of Newent, a chicken producer in Gloucestershire, a county in England's South West. The firm was once a struggling local producer, but today is one of the country's largest after teaming with a local Muslim businessman and supplying halal chickens to Nando's, a fast-food chain popular among the Muslim community. That provides the firm with an ideal base from which to venture into the East's fast-growing Muslim markets.

The upshot is that the potential market size is large. My estimates put consumer spending by Muslims in the East alone at around $2,500 billion, a figure that includes consumption by Muslims living in non-Muslim countries, and also before considering sales to Muslims in the West or non-Muslim customers.[16] These are big dollars, and while the Muslim market has its challenges, it will be tough for most companies to ignore as they look for the next source of growth, especially given the expected growth in the Muslim world's still-young population over the coming decades.

Indeed, what makes the Muslim consumer especially attractive is the fact that the Muslim world is young and many Muslim countries are still developing, meaning that consumers are often buying branded products for the first time. This provides companies with an opportunity to build brand loyalty, rather than having to convince consumers to switch later in life, unlike in older and more mature markets such as America and Europe and even increasingly in China, where the average consumer is 35 years old and can select from a growing range of local and foreign brands. For those companies looking for the next China, the Muslim world demands attention.

4

BOLLYWOOD STARS AND INDONESIAN PUNK ROCK

A FLOURISHING LOCAL ENTERTAINMENT INDUSTRY

MADHURI DIXIT STARED STRAIGHT INTO THE CAMERA WITH A SULTRY look as the wind ruffled her hair before she launched into a song-and-dance spectacular surrounded by a chorus of young women. The young men in the cinema stamped their feet and yelled in delight. Watching a Bollywood film is pure exhilaration. It is even better when watching at the famous Raj Mandir Cinema in the northwestern Indian town of Jaipur. This single-screen cinema is a postmodern pink structure from the outside, but built like an opera house on the inside with a grand stairway, crenellated balconies, and gold trimming. The Raj Mandir echoes Hollywood's Golden Age, when actors such as Clark Gable and Bette Davis ruled the screen and cinema was at the height of its popularity.

The young men had paid $1.50 for tickets right up close to the screen. I had opted for the $4.00 seats in the less adventurous upper balcony along with middle-class Indian families. The film was not dubbed into English, but the plot was easy to understand with the film's feast of themes—love, despair, cruelty, and redemption—all packed into two hours. I took my warm samosa out of an oily paper bag, drank my Thums Up, and settled in to enjoy the catchy songs and spectacular dance routines. I'm a fan of watching the latest Bollywood film on long-haul flights, but there's a world of difference between a six-inch screen and one of India's 10,000 single-screen theaters.

Of course, many don't agree. "Sure, it's fun for a few nights. But really, most of us would choose the comfort of an air-conditioned multiplex given the choice," says the more experienced Jehil Thakkar, KPMG's Mumbai-based Head of Media and Entertainment.

And he makes a strong case. The Inox Multiplex cinema in Mumbai's Nariman Point is typical of the country's 1,700 multiplex screens. On a Friday night in early 2013, I sat through *Raanjhanaa* surrounded by couples and families who had paid $6.00 for a ticket. It was certainly less atmospheric than a single-screen cinema, but admittedly more comfortable. I could also choose from five different films with multiple showing times. The Raj Mandir offered just two films, each showing twice a day. That's fine if you visit the cinema just a few times a year, but more of a problem for those who visit monthly, or who don't like the small selection of films that month.

Bollywood is an old business. Its roots date back to at least the 1930s, and the industry produces more films than Hollywood each year, even if the country's box office is smaller. Yet the differences between the Raj Mandir and the Inox Multiplex also illustrate how the industry is evolving rapidly as a commercial opportunity.

It's tempting to ask when Bollywood will emerge as a major global player. When will it take on Hollywood? But those are also the wrong questions. It's like asking when Chinese companies will start building out retail chain or distribution networks in America and Europe. The reality is that Bollywood's major market isn't overseas in developed markets, but at home and among its near neighbors—Bangladesh, Pakistan, the Middle East. That's where the real growth opportunities are: populations are bigger, purchasing power is growing rapidly, and Bollywood is selling to a culturally similar audience.

The film *Raanjhanaa* neatly captures some of the changes in Bollywood. *Raanjhanaa* is a terrific romantic drama about the son of a Tamil priest and a Muslim girl living in the city of Varanasi. It is also the debut for the actor Dhanush, who played the film's lead male role and happens to be one of the biggest stars of Tamil cinema. To the outsider, it is easy to assume that Bollywood is India's film industry, and yet Hindi-speaking Bollywood films account for less than half of the films produced each year. The Tamil film industry based around the southern city of Chennai is just one of Bollywood's competitors among more than a dozen major film industries all using India's local dialects.

Indeed, in central Mumbai, Tamil film fans celebrate the opening of each new film by Tamil superstar Rajinikanth by bathing 30-foot-tall cutouts of the man in fresh milk. As if that weren't enough, a celluloid copy of the film itself is placed on an altar in its canister, much like the statue of a Hindu god. The screaming crowds outside of Hollywood's Chinese Theatre or El Capitan Theatre are impressive, but take a look at YouTube clips of Tamil fans: they explain not only India's passion for films, but also the type of competition Bollywood faces in its own market.

Thakkar tells a story about how economics are changing India's film industry. "The rise of the multiplex has helped drive the growth in local films. Higher incomes mean higher ticket prices, and so production budgets have risen, making local films more enjoyable to watch. Even the single-screens are charging higher prices," he says.[1]

His reference to "the multiplex" is one I heard repeatedly across the region in subsequent months. In India, the number of multiplex screens has grown to about 1,700 in the past few years.[2] They allow cinemas to experiment with different pricing models, especially during the opening week and weekend, which now account for 60 to 80 percent of a film's box-office revenue, much as it might in the United States. Just as the multiplex saved America's film industry in the 1960s from the rise of television and, later, DVDs, it is changing India's film industry and challenging the traditional dominance of Bollywood films.

And it's not just the multiplexes. "Ten years ago the local production houses had to rely entirely on ticket sales, but today they are earning 40 percent of their income from television sales, as well as music rights," Thakkar adds. The income is attractive enough that films are often televised just 60 to 90 days after their cinema release.[3]

The result is that India has an increasingly vibrant local film market—Tamil, Telagu, Kanada, or Tamala, to name a few. "There's even been a revival of regional cinema in Bengal and northern India," says Thakkar. Films often have native grassroots themes that appeal to local audiences. However, it also helps that local films are cheaper to produce at just $150,000 to $600,000 for a typical Marathi or Punjabi movie versus $2 million to $20 million for a Bollywood movie. Local firms also have longer theatrical releases, opening in 20 to 30 screens in the first week, then 60 to 70 screens in the second week.[4]

Bollywood is responding in turn. "Production houses are looking to de-risk from Hindi films, partly attracted by what's happening in the local film industry," adds Thakkar. The idea of Bollywood de-risking by going local, rather than international, neatly sums up how the East is increasingly looking inward for growth opportunities.

Indeed, the changes create a challenging environment for the American studios. Most of the big studios have set up shop in Mumbai over the past decade, hoping to tap into the industry's growing box-office revenues. At first, they simply dubbed Hollywood films into Hindi and local languages, hoping that what sold in America would also sell in India. But that strategy struggled, and Hollywood films account for just 10 percent of India's box office today. Take the Inox Multiplex in Nariman Point on my Friday night visit. Sure, Brad Pitt's *World War Z* was showing. But everything else was in Hindi.

"What tends to work are action flicks, disaster flicks, superhero flicks. Stallone, Schwarzenegger are familiar brands and so easy marketing. But not comedy or drama; these either aren't released, or only for a limited Westernized audience," says Thakkar.

Realizing their mistake, the foreign studios changed their strategy and are instead teaming up with locals to make films: Disney purchased UTV, a large Indian film and television group; Viacom, the American conglomerate, has a joint venture with TV18, an Indian media company. The UTV acquisition was a particularly smart move given that the studio has produced a number of recent hits, including *Barfi,* a quirky romantic comedy with a wonderful opening chase scene. And yet the studio's movies continue to be promoted under the UTV brand. Even the firm's commercial material has surprisingly little reference to its ultimate owners, the all-powerful Disney.

It is a remarkable change: the powerful American studios have come to India and then turned local, leveraging their management and technical expertise, rather than their brands, in order to generate a new revenue stream and de-risk from Hollywood, much as Bollywood itself is de-risking by producing local films.

To be fair, their arrival is shaking up Bollywood. Even now, most of Bollywood's studios and production companies are run as family-owned businesses. Their facilities and offices are spread over Mumbai's northern suburbs. The most successful actors are found in the wealthier neighborhoods of Bandra and Juhu, the studios farther north in the emerging suburbs of Goregaon and Andheri. It is in Andheri where Bollywood hopefuls are most likely to be found in the suburb's many coffee shops, meeting with casting agents or hoping to be discovered as they hang out.

Tanaaz Bhatia's office lies in the Santacruz district, a short drive from the offices of Shahrukh Khan, one of Bollywood's biggest superstars, and also a short distance from a local slum. (The rich and famous and Mumbai's poor are often neighbors, even if their daily lives are worlds apart.) The two-story office is squeezed next to a residential apartment building; its front wall is covered in old Bollywood film posters and so is easy to spot from the street. Inside, the place hums as staff work in small offices from which they plot the marketing and merchandising of India's next box-office hit, for ticket sales and television income are not the only source of growing revenues.

Bhatia is CEO and Founder of Bottomline Media. A Mumbai native, she cut her teeth working for Merrill Lynch as an investment banker in the entertainment sector in New York City, later returning to her hometown, recognizing the opportunity to bring best practices from the United States to India's film business.

"There are untapped opportunities," Bhatia says.[5] "Indian production houses are only just learning about merchandising and promotional tie-ups, and so we work with them right from the scripting process through to production and finally marketing. It helps to lower their overall production costs." She points to the pens, mugs, and board games that fill her small office. Many are emblazoned with the chiseled features of Shahrukh Khan and are advertising *Ra.One*, the superhero film. "*Ra.One* was a big deal for us. We were the first to create a nation-wide McDonald's Happy Meal based on *Ra.One* and gave out little Happy Meal toys. We also collaborated with Sony and created the first PlayStation game based on an Indian film."

"The international brands understand that the only way to break into the local market is by identifying with something local. And who better than a Shahrukh Khan or a Salman Khan? These merchandising and promotional opportunities aren't new to Hollywood, but they are new to Bollywood," Bhatia says.

However, merchandising doesn't yet sell in India as it does in America. "The pirated market is really large. No one really goes out to buy this stuff. But if you give it away free, then people will happily take it, such as a Happy Meal toy. Or you have to make it easily affordable, like a 5 rupee pen," says Bhatia. Promotional activities also offer Western multinationals a new channel for tapping into India's consumer class. Western Union, the American financial services company, tied up with *Ra.One* to promote its services. The slogan, *There's a superhero in you. Send money through Western Union,* ran in the company's print advertisements, while the company's television commercial ran globally.

The tie-up between films, merchandising, and promotional activities will only make India's film industry even more central to the country's growing commercial opportunities. Rather than look abroad, Bollywood will understandably look to its own rapidly changing markets as demand for local films rises and opportunities to sell merchandising grow. For the foreign studios the complexity is even greater as they try to find the right model for tapping into the country's demand, and the logic of tying up with a local production house and producing films with local actors will only grow.

THERE IS GOOD REASON FOR HOLLYWOOD TO GET ITS STRATEGY RIGHT IN India and elsewhere in the region. Not only is the international box office bigger relative to the American market, it is also growing more rapidly. Moreover, the biggest gains are in the East, where the region's box office is a big driver of Hollywood's growth.

Figures from the Motion Picture Association of America show that the international box office was worth $24 billion in 2012, with receipts rising by around $1.5 billion each year for the previous five years.[6] By contrast, the combined American and Canadian box office was worth just half that at $10.8 billion. The figures are reflected in Hollywood's financial performance. In 2012, the six major American studios took 62 percent of their gross box office from overseas ticket sales.[7] The reliance of the six studios on foreign box office was also relatively consistent: Fox had the highest dependence at 73 percent and Disney the lowest at a nevertheless still high 57 percent.[8]

The studios can expect to see those numbers continue to rise steadily over the coming decade. The implication is that the Hollywood studios are behaving no differently than any other big multinational and following the global money trail, and that trail leads to the East. The region already accounts for half of the global box office, and its faster rate of growth suggests, by rough straight-line estimates, that the East's box office will overtake the United States in just a few years as a larger source of box-office receipts for the six major American studios. In short, the studios will care more about finding a box-office hit for Indian or Korean audiences than for American ones.

The region's real giant, however, is China. Not only is China's box office worth $2.7 billion, as compared to India's $1.4 billion, but Hollywood captured 53 percent of China's box office in 2012 compared to 10 percent of India's.[9] Hollywood's suited moneymen have a rightful obsession with Chinese filmgoers.

So far, the message is that superhero and action films work, explaining why Hollywood has been churning these films out in such large numbers. In 2013, the top-grossing foreign films in India included *Iron Man 3*, *Fast and Furious 6*, *Man of Steel*, and *The Croods*. In China, the top-grossing films included *Iron Man 3*, *Skyfall*, *The Croods*, and *Star Trek into Darkness*. It might also explain the resurrection of ageing 1980s action stars, such as Sylvester Stallone and Arnold Schwarzenegger, who are popular brand names in the developing world. (The Stallone-directed *The Expendables 2* made more money from international sales than Steven Spielberg's *Lincoln* made in America.)[10]

The challenge, though, is sustaining that effort, especially in the face of a flourishing domestic film industry. To be fair, Hollywood accounts for a similarly large share of the box office in Korea and France, at around 50 percent for both markets. But what if India is the more likely trajectory for China, rather than Korea and France?

Central to this question is whether Chinese audiences are watching Hollywood films by preference or because of a lack of choice. Bollywood has an 80-year history, and Indian film producers are relatively free to choose their subjects. By contrast, the Cultural Revolution suffocated China's film industry for a period, and regulators still tightly control film content, banning politically sensitive subjects. In the past decade, a handful of directors, such as Zhang Yimou and Feng Xianggang, have directed lavish films, but there has been a lack of smaller directors creating real hits. What happens when China starts producing more of the type of films that Chinese audiences want to see?

"Hollywood films have driven the growth of China's cinema industry. And yet, they've suffered a clear decline in 2013," says Robert Cain, CEO of Pacific Bridge Pictures.[11] He is speaking by phone from California, but has spent over 20 years in China, Hong Kong, and Taiwan helping to develop and launch cross-border entertainment ventures.

"It's still too early to know why. The audience might be looking for local language films, wanting local stories and faces. They may also be tired of seeing the same Hollywood films," he says. "You also can't discount the importance of restrictions. The film regulators really manage the business. They choose the release dates, the quality of the screens, and the ability of foreign films to advertise." The fact that *The Dark Knight Rises* and *The Amazing Spider-Man* were forced to open on the same weekend across China in 2012, as were *The Lorax* and *Ice Age: Continental Drift*, is just one trick the regulators can play to dampen Hollywood's sales.

And yet *Iron Man 3* enjoyed unusual government support, according to Cain, when it opened in 2013 and still barely edged out the local romantic drama, *So Young*. The latter admittedly enjoyed a head start heading into the May holiday, again helped by the regulators. But its performance was impressive nevertheless. The film was based on the Chinese young-adult novel *To Our Eventually Lost Youth* and was cast on a relatively small budget. *Lost in Thailand*, a story of three bumbling Chinese tourists in Thailand that echoed the best of Hong Kong slapstick comedy and had me laughing on the flight to Mumbai, did similarly well. Might blame lie with the limited number of high-quality local releases?

Raymond Zhou is the Beijing-based film critic for *China Daily*, and having studied at the University of California, Los Angeles (UCLA), he is familiar with both the American and the Chinese markets. "In the past decade, China has relied on established directors. We adopted a big movie strategy to counter Hollywood. The movies were mainly costume dramas, epic movies with big budgets. But the big movies have more recently flopped. Not just one movie, but many."[12] Lu Chuan's *The Last Supper* is just one example of what Raymond is referring to: the lavish costume drama was produced on a budget of around $15 million, but made significantly less than that at the box office.

"But in the past 12 months, a revolution has happened. These small-budget movies, like *Lost in Thailand*, are made by first-time directors and have done so well. It's a big surprise. Everyone is scratching their heads trying to understand the formula. But these films tackle subjects that are out of Hollywood's comfort zone."

"The mushrooming of multiplexes in second- and third-tier cities is also changing the dynamic. Audiences in smaller cities are not as familiar with Hollywood movies, and might be more comfortable with a local movie," Zhou adds. It's an important point as the number of multiplexes in these smaller or inland cities has grown steadily in the past few years. Zhong Ying Xing Mei, for instance, is one of the country's largest multiplex operators with cinemas in nearly 200 locations across the country, of which some 112 are in third- and fourth-tier cities, most located in the country's inland regions.[13]

If local movies are gaining ground, then the American studios look much like the foreign multinationals did in the 1990s when they enjoyed a first-mover advantage and gained dominant market share in China—from Procter & Gamble, Nike, and McDonald's. But eventually the local competition stiffens up and does a better job of catering to local tastes. (And it's much harder to produce a film that suits local interests than it is to create a running shoe.) In that event, the American film studios might have to tackle China much as they do India, co-producing with the local studios, working with local directors, or simply acquiring films and distributing them.

Indeed, India's experience offers a warning for Hollywood. For a start, Bollywood has excelled at producing films that tell local jokes for local audiences. Take *Bol Bachan* or *OMG—Oh My God*. Both films have a slapstick style that is similar to China's *Lost in Thailand*. Much like *Lost in Thailand*, both films were also a smash at the box office and outperformed Hollywood's toughest competitors—*The Avengers*, *The Dark Knight Rises*, and *The Amazing Spider-Man*. Further, the success of small-budget films catering to local tastes is threatening Bollywood much as small-budget films are challenging China's established directors, and Hollywood will also need to respond.

For the last word I turned to Tony Ngai, Marketing Manager of Salon Films in Hong Kong. I had met Ngai in 2012 while preparing a commercial strategy for a large American theatrical business wanting to enter China. What makes Ngai special is his perspective. He joined Salon Films in 1969 and has observed Hong Kong's industry evolve over 40 years. Today, the company is one of the region's largest film-equipment rental companies, but it got its break when it beat the much larger Shaw Brothers Studios as the sole Hong Kong distributor for Panavision in the 1970s, and Ngai subsequently spent several years in Los Angeles training to use the equipment.

I met Ngai again in the summer of 2013 to talk about my work. The company's facilities are in Kowloon near the old airport, in one of the city's many 15-story industrial buildings. Visitors take the building's jumbo-sized warehouse elevators to an office packed with lights, dollies, and camera equipment, where Ngai is waiting.

"In those days, the Shaw Brothers were producing a portion of movies to a template: hiring Japanese directors, copying Japanese production styles, producing mainly Kung Fu movies," he says.[14] "But that all changed in the early 1970s with a new wave of films. The directors were new to film, but not to the industry itself. They had cut their teeth producing dramas for the local television stations like TVB or CTV and so had a good sense of what the audience wanted. It was fast and scientific audience research." Ngai marks Hong Kong's film industry growth from that period as, all of a sudden, the audience had a choice.

I am struck by his comments. That shift from template filmmaking to producing local films that identify with local audiences was an important step for Hong Kong's film industry. It certainly works in India. Might the same be true in China? Might the industry be shifting from the big-budget template model to local filmmaking?

THE IMPORTANCE OF LOCAL TASTES TO SUCCESS IN THE ENTERTAINMENT industry is critical. There are very few examples of crossover productions that work. I put the question of crossovers to Thakkar, Bhatia, Cain, Zhou, and Ngai, and got a similar response each time—it's all down to luck rather than strategic design.

The challenge is that there are few local tastes that have a genuinely international market. The superhero film is perhaps one of the rare examples. Sport is another. Consider the 700 million people who watch soccer's World Cup every four years. One of the more unusual examples is India's recent impact on cricket. Cricket isn't an easy sport to explain. Try convincing an American or a German that it's possible to play a single match over five days that ends in a draw and yet still attracts an audience. Test cricket, or the longest form of the game, is a historical anomaly, somehow escaping the relentless drive to make sports more action-packed.

My wife, who is from Hong Kong, has always struggled. But she certainly appreciates the passion for the sport after a short stay in New Delhi in 2010. Australia was playing India at the time, and I was watching the game on television in our hotel room when we had some room service delivered. The waiter was a young man in his early 20s and was dressed in a hotel uniform. He entered the room, set up the food, and then saw the game on television. He promptly sat down on the edge of our bed and started to debate with me the merits of the Australian team, throwing in more anecdotes, statistics, and biographical details than even I knew about my own team.

I was impressed. But so was my wife, who watched the conversation in amazement. I shrugged my shoulders in reply to her unasked question. "That's cricket. And that's how India feels about the game."

India's passion for cricket has translated into billions of dollars. Sunil Gavaskar, a famous Indian player from the 1970s, writes in his autobiography *Sunny Days* how teammates devoured biscuits served at county matches in England to save money on meals.[15] Today's cricketers earn considerably more. Sachin Tendulkar, for instance, was estimated to have earned $22 million from endorsements and playing fees in a country where wages are just a few thousand dollars.[16] The faces of today's cricketing stars stare out from advertising billboards across the country, and the sport generates hundreds of millions in advertising revenues.

And while Bollywood hasn't turned the global film industry upside down, India's passion for cricket has certainly had an indelible impact on the sport wherever it is played—from Australia to New Zealand to South Africa, and, of course, England, all developed countries with strong cricketing cultures.

The earthquake came in 2008, when Lalit Modi and the Board of Control for Cricket in India (BCCI) created the Indian Premier League (IPL), based on a short form of the match that lasted 20-overs a side, or around three hours. Ten city-based franchises, such as the Rajasthan Royals and Chennai Super Kings, were sold to bidders that included Bollywood stars. The IPL's brilliance, though, was in allowing each franchise to bid for up to 11 foreign players at an annual auction, paying large sums of money to attract the world's cricketing stars—from Australia's Shane Warne, England's Andrew Flintoff, and the West Indies' Brian Lara—effectively making the league a showcase for the world's best players.

Man Jit Singh, CEO of Sony Entertainment India, was critical to the sport's inception. "We all took a huge risk in setting up the IPL. It was an unknown format. But it was executed very well," he said when we met at his office in Mumbai's Malad West in the summer of 2013. "The organizers used the best examples from leagues around the world, such as the English Premier League or NBA. It was the first time India had seen cheerleaders; it was the first time Indian stadiums provided world-class facilities so that companies would feel comfortable inviting their clients and vendors to matches. We also put the matches on Sony's biggest channel in India—a Hindi movie channel that has three times the reach of any sports channel."[17]

But it was the heady mix of cricket and Bollywood that provided rocket fuel for the sport's success. Bollywood film stars even owned teams: Shahrukh Khan, for example, purchased the Kolkata Knight Riders franchise. Having worked in Los Angeles for 30 years, Singh understood the power of film and sport. "It was a deliberate decision to have a glamour quotient, and the organizers were approaching Bollywood stars throughout the process. Many didn't want to touch it, as there was no track record. But those who did have since done well. And now there are stars attending every game. It's like having Jack Nicholson sitting on center court at a Los Angeles Lakers game," Singh says.

I asked him, "When did you know it would be a success?" "We are only a week into the first season and I saw the type of crowds and the way they received the matches. Then the ratings came out and we knew we had a great success. Soon advertisers were lining up at the door," Singh replied after some thought.

It is the IPL's marketing reach that explains its financial power. "IPL is a unique concept that arrived at the right time. It appeals to a younger population that wants a faster game and combines our only truly national sport with Bollywood," says Singh. "It also appeals to every income level. Only 65 percent of Indians have televisions. And there will be crowds watching the game outside tea shops during the final stages of a tense match." That translates into strong dollar revenues. Pepsi-Cola is the IPL's current sponsor, but Vodafone, Samsung, and Hindustan Unilever are just a few of the big multinationals advertising during the event, among a range of local companies.

If those advertising revenues continue to increase alongside the country's growing consumer market, then the fees paid to foreign players will also continue to rise with implications for the global sport. In fact, tensions are already emerging, especially among disgruntled English players. The English cricket authorities require their players to return midway through the seven-week IPL tournament because of domestic match commitments. By contrast, the Australian authorities allow their players to participate as the tournament takes place during the Australian layoff season, although they will privately advise those at risk of injury to take a vacation instead.

In 2013, some 33 Australian players participated in the IPL, with 13 newly auctioned players earning an average $375,000. By contrast, only four English players participated as they offered a much lower return on investment for franchise owners. This was at a time when the English national team was higher ranked than the Australian.

That has created tensions between English players and the sport's national authorities. English wicketkeeper Matt Prior was one of those disgruntled players who went unsold at the 2013 auction. He was quoted afterwards as saying that English players are becoming "frustrated" at the scheduling conflict. "I'm employed by the ECB, so I do what the ECB says right now." He continued, "The IPL and these 20 competitions are not going away. People love them and the players enjoy playing in them, so there are going to be more and more people getting frustrated at the lack of opportunity to play in the IPL. So things may have to change in time."[18]

Cricket players earn far less than other sportsmen, especially those in the United States. But just imagine if the NBA's Kobe Bryant or the NFL's Tom Brady publicly complained about the lack of opportunity to play in India rather than in their respective American leagues—that's the impact IPL has had on cricket.

I left Singh's office and headed back toward the center of town, my car fighting its way through the afternoon traffic as the monsoon rains clogged the streets. I picked up a Mumbai Indians team shirt at an official Adidas outlet not far from the team's Churchgate Stadium. At $40 the shirts were pricey. You could buy a similar LA Lakers shirt for half the price. "Do they sell?" I asked the sales staff. "When the teams are playing, that's almost all we sell" was the reply. The company had given the young man some corporate tickets to attend a Mumbai Indians match that year. "It was great," he said, a big grin on his face. "Mumbai Indians!"

YOU WOULD THINK THAT THE MUSIC INDUSTRY WOULD HAVE AN EASIER TIME of it compared to the film industry. After all, a song lasts around two to three minutes, rather than 90 to 120. There is also a better balance between words and music—the music industry is full of songs that have succeeded in spite of dire lyrics. The rapid ascent of K-pop, or Korean pop music, doesn't have a comparable parallel in the film industry. Chinese, Hindi, or even French-language films have a niche market overseas, but they have never captured such attention in the same way K-pop has in Asia, especially among the youth market.

"K-pop is a miracle," says Cherry Leong over dim sum at a restaurant in Hong Kong's Kowloon district.[19] We sit on one side of the restaurant's oversized round tables as waiters efficiently bustle around. Leong is Director of the International Pop Department for Universal Music Hong Kong, responsible for marketing the firm's international music.

"Foreign-language acts shouldn't work," she warns me. So what makes K-pop successful? "They work hard to promote their acts. They are very well trained in dancing and singing, plus they are very hard-working. Psy recently signed to Republic Records and is distributed by Universal Music. He is always touring the region and just performed in Paris at the Eiffel Tower. Some of the K-pop stars are even publishing songs in Japanese in order to break into the market. That's why J-pop is struggling," she adds, referring to Japanese pop. "It was huge in the 1980s, but they aren't interested in exporting and Japanese artists just aren't big on performing outside Japan," says Leong.

Throughout the next two hours, Leong provides me with a 101 course on music industry promotion. It sounds like a tough business and without a simple template for success. "We have to work harder than ever to promote our acts. YouTube, Facebook, WeChat, and Weibo, all the main social media channels. And you have to grow each foreign artist locally. You can't assume that what's big in America will automatically play well here." The hard work shows, judging by Leong's Facebook page. It's a constant stream of updates on local promotional events, YouTube videos, and other sound bites.

There are exceptions, of course. "Taylor Swift and Justin Bieber are huge in Hong Kong, but there have been few hits since them. The big acts also only work if they are 'idolish.' They have to attract the young kids." Swift and Bieber are part of Leong's portfolio, and she was tasked with helping Bieber on his recent visit to Hong Kong.

And that's the challenge. Even for a major label such as Universal, there are only a few Taylor Swifts and Justin Biebers able to sell their music on the basis of their global appeal. Otherwise, foreign artists need to be developed locally in each market, irrespective of whether they are American, British, or Korean. Talking with Leong, I am reminded that the success of the low-budget Chinese films *Lost in Thailand* and *So*

Young owed more to social media than to a deliberate and expensive marketing campaign. And as the region's music industry develops, the competition is only getting tougher.

Take the Chinese music industry. "Many of the mainland artists don't do well in Hong Kong, especially the northern Chinese acts," Leong says. "The main reason is the cultural differences between northern and southern China. The differences in language and even accents are also important," she says, referring to the wide variety of dialects spoken across the country. The differences between Cantonese and Mandarin are naturally large. But even variations in culture and accent between Cantonese-speaking populations can matter for Hong Kong's young music fans.

"That said, I have one artist, Wanting, who is really grabbing attention. She was born in Harbin, but then moved to Canada when she was 16 to study." I ask about the name Wanting. "It's a play on her Chinese name, Wan Ting. It works well in both languages," Leong replies.

"She started out by giving her CDs to bars and coffee shops in Beijing. But she got her real break when one of her songs was included on a movie soundtrack, and the film's success created a lot of good publicity for Wanting," she says. That soundtrack was for the Hong Kong film *Love in the Buff* and the song was titled "Drenched." The film's director heard the song playing in a coffee shop in Beijing where they were working on the script and reached out to Wanting. Her career flourished soon after and included an appearance on the state broadcaster CCTV's New Year Gala in 2013.

Nevertheless, Wanting, K-pop, and Justin Bieber are exceptions to the general rule. Indeed, the language barrier is also a challenge for local acts. Just consider Indonesia, where Bahasa is spoken widely for commercial and political purposes, but dozens of dialects are used locally across the long archipelago.

And that's a challenge for the country's music stars. My wife's family is originally Chinese Indonesian and many relatives still live in the country. Her cousin's husband also happens to be one of Bali's biggest pop stars: his first album was released in 1996 and sold more than 60,000 copies. Widi Widiana is a gentle-spoken guy with a long ponytail. Walk around Denpasar with Widiana and there are the inevitable stares from shop assistants and passersby as they recognize his face. His music videos often feature Widiana strumming a guitar or walking along a beach, crooning romantic songs. But always in the Balinese dialect.

That is a deliberate choice by Widiana, who is the son of a temple priest and sings in a traditional form of Balinese that makes him popular among the young who find the language more emotionally rich, as well as the old who are pleased in the respect the songs show for the island's traditions. But it also means that Widiana is singing largely for a Balinese audience and has rarely tried to sell his albums outside of Bali in spite of his local fame. He once recorded in Jakarta for a compilation album. But rather than singing an original Balinese song, he performed the Bahasa translation of a Chinese original.

Some Balinese bands are big across Indonesia. The Bali-based Superman Is Dead is the best example. The country's biggest punk-rock band has a loyal, albeit niche, following across the country. "But the band started singing in Bahasa since 2003," says Wendi Putranto, Deputy Editor of *Rolling Stone* magazine.[20]

The Rolling Stone Café in Jakarta is the magazine's only venue outside of Hong Kong. I arrive just before the rains start and move up to the second floor with a view over two soundstages. The place has a well-worn feel during the day, the slightly grubby feeling left behind by a sweating crowd the night before. Putranto has the look of a hard-core music fan. Wearing a black T-shirt and thick black glasses, he talks comfortably about the changes in Indonesia's music industry over the decades, not least the recent election of Joko Widodo, Jakarta's relatively youthful and progressive governor.

"He's a metal-head," says Putranto proudly. The mayor had to give up a guitar given to him by Metallica, the American heavy metal band, in early 2013 for fears of corruption, but only after first having his picture taken by the local press while he strummed the guitar lovingly. Widodo was also a fan of Led Zeppelin, Deep Purple, and Napalm Death.

But he wasn't typical of the average Indonesian music fan. "When we first started publishing *Rolling Stone* magazine, I reckon foreign bands accounted for about 60 percent of our stories and Indonesia bands just 40 percent. But that's now reversed with Indonesia bands accounting for 60 percent." He goes on to explain that the real change began in the mid-1990s. "This was the start of a golden era. It was because of Suharto's fall," he says, referring to the late Indonesian president. "It opened up the country to new possibilities. In the '80s, the radio stations only played foreign music, but that all changed after Suharto."

The growth of the local music industry might be due in part to political change. But success is still hard work, even for the country's Bahasa-language acts. Putranto goes on to explain what it takes to succeed in Indonesia, describing a situation not all that different from Leong's challenges in Hong Kong.

For a start, social media are increasingly critical. Take Superman Is Dead. I later download the band's *Black Market Love* album on iTunes for $10.00. It's a punchy mix of rock anthems. But iTunes was just the latest iteration of the band's online strategy, and the band's history was a roadmap of the rise of online media. "They started out with Yahoo Groups in the early 2000s, with fans swapping information on the band, and then moved to Friendster in 2004," says Putranto. Today, they have active Facebook and Twitter accounts and their music videos are easily available on YouTube.

It helps that Indonesia has nearly 30 million smartphone users, with the number rising rapidly,[21] not to mention some 52 million Facebook accounts and many using Twitter,[22] making a social media campaign a critical part of any marketing strategy, and the band has admirably evolved alongside new technologies.

Still, Superman Is Dead also tours regularly. "From Aceh to Sulawesi," says Putranto. "Most artists make their money through concerts. There's too many illegal downloads in Indonesia. But touring is also expensive. Indonesia is an archipelago and that makes it tough traveling between cities and venues." A quick look at Superman Is Dead's website in my hotel later that night showed that the band had toured Surabaya, Yogyakarta, Cianjur, Malang, Denpasar, Mataran, Lombok, and Gresik since the start of the year, sticking largely to the bigger cities on Java, but nevertheless moving about regularly.

There are other channels. "You can hire Colonel Sanders as your agent," he laughs. The American fast-food chain KFC has been selling CDs in Indonesia since 2007. They only sell local bands, and often amateurs, which is a good shot in the arm for the local music industry. "A mainstream artist can sell 500,000 to 2 million copies that way," Putranto says. "It's chicken and a CD." It also overcomes the problems of selling CDs at all given the problem of illegal downloads. Again, it's not a strategy that might appeal to the biggest foreign stars, but for a local artist it's a great way to expand your fan base.

I said goodbye to Putranto, and headed back to the center of town. Near my hotel, I stopped at a KFC to buy my "chicken and a CD." Not recognizing any of the artists on sale, and standing there plagued by indecision, I plumped for an album by Sammy Simorangkir on the advice of a young teenage girl next to me. It turns out Sammy was a bit of a bad boy, earlier being picked up by police for stealing a car and drug use—true rock-star pedigree. Sammy doesn't appear to be in prison for his misdemeanors since his agency had helpfully provided their contact details on the back of the CD for anyone wanting to make event bookings. Colonel Sanders was clearly doing his job.

THE EAST'S ENTERTAINMENT INDUSTRY IS WONDERFULLY DIVERSE, FROM India's Bollywood dance spectaculars to China's low-budget rom-coms to Indonesia's punk-rock bands. But if there is a single thread running through the region, it is the rise of a more local industry catering to local tastes. The big global entertainment events are still able to blast their way into local markets—whether it's *The Dark Knight Rises* or Justin Bieber. But they are small in number. Even for local entertainment events there are challenges related to regional differences—such as those faced by Bollywood's Hindi films or Indonesia's Balinese-speaking Widi Widiana.

For foreign entertainment companies, the challenge is even greater as they try to tap into the region's increasingly robust entertainment industries. Trying to develop films or acts with a global appeal is incredibly challenging—we are still waiting for the next Justin Bieber. Moreover, audiences may soon tire of certain products that are repeated endlessly with little variation—how many more superhero films can the world really watch? Crossover productions aren't a simple alternative—for every *Life of Pi* or *Crouching Tiger, Hidden Dragon*, there are many more like *Big Shot's Funeral* or *Karate Kid*.

Most likely the entertainment industry will simply follow the same path as other multinationals that have already recognized the challenges: consider Unilever's success in selling Lakmé-branded cosmetics or Kissan-branded jams and ketchups, all local products for a local market that rarely sell in America or Europe.

The rise of the online media will only accelerate the change by allowing unknown actors, directors, and musicians to break into the national scene without the backing of a large foreign entertainment company to support them. The low-budget Chinese film *So Young* is just one example. The Bali-based punk-rock band Superman Is Dead is another. These are acts that know their local markets and can respond nimbly to changes in popular culture. And the time Universal Music's Cherry Leong must spend on Facebook and other online media to build support for her acts illustrates just how grassroots even the world's biggest entertainment companies will have to go.

Indeed, the music studios were perhaps fastest to adapt given the relative simplicity of signing a local artist: take Universal Music Hong Kong, where the company's list includes local stars Eason Chan and Kelvin Kwan, or the fact that Sony BMG Indonesia signed Superman Is Dead. But the film industry is also catching up: consider Disney-UTV's role in the smash hit *Chennai Express*. Hollywood's big box-office share in China has perhaps delayed the same adjustment, especially given its success in other markets, such as Korea and France. But if India is the better guide, then Hollywood might find itself making fewer superhero films and instead signing up to help fund and co-produce more Chinese films.

5

——

CHINA GOES GLOBAL, AGAIN

A NEW PHASE FOR CHINESE OUTBOUND INVESTMENT

Tony Shi was speaking about his recent trip to Brazil as we sat opposite each other in Alfies, the restaurant in Dunhill's flagship store on Hong Kong's Connaught Road. I thought I traveled regularly, but Shi had collected some serious air miles visiting America, Europe, Argentina, Russia, Poland, Ukraine, South Africa, Algeria, Saudi Arabia, and the UAE in the past year. As the Beijing-based head of International Business Development for Foton, one of China's largest state-owned automobile manufacturers, Shi was in the vanguard of China's overseas expansion and so had good reason to travel.[1]

"Don't worry about the price," he said. "It's been a great year for us. We've made good money and need to spend it. It's either that or build more factories," he joked.

Chinese state firms have made some impressive global gains in the past decade. In 2012, the Fortune Global 500 ranked three Chinese firms, including two state oil companies, Sinopec and China National Petroleum, as well as the country's largest power distribu- tor, State Grid, among the world's ten largest firms by revenues. And they were not exceptions as Chinese firms made up almost one-fifth of the entire list with 87 companies in total, their global businesses growing as they took stakes in a range of overseas assets, including American energy companies, Brazilian oil firms, and Australian min- ing groups.

But then the state sector had also enjoyed a great decade at home. Most firms were restructured during the late 1990s through a Darwinian policy that sacrificed weak performers and encouraged the strongest to grow even bigger. Riding a ten-year economic boom, the surviving firms subsequently generated huge profits and paid out only a small fraction in dividends. The government's nearly $700 billion fiscal stimulus package during the global financial crisis was like throwing gasoline on a fire as state banks pumped cash into state firms and policy planners rubber-stamped huge infrastructure plans.

By contrast, life was tougher for the country's private firms. I recall one conversation with a privately owned battery manufacturer based in the southern suburbs of Guangzhou. He had started the company in the 1990s owning little more than a bicycle. When I met him, he had factories in Brazil and India and enjoyed strong sales growth in Africa and the Middle East. A model company, you might think, and one that the country's banks would be keen to do business with. But when I asked about bank loans, he laughed and shook his head: "Not even we can get loans. Everything is self-funded."

It was a common complaint among the country's private entrepre- neurs. In 2012, the China Council for the Promotion of International

Trade surveyed nearly 400 Chinese firms to understand why they were expanding abroad: a majority of private firms claimed to be disappointed by their sales and profitability and over two-thirds cited the difficulty of getting loans from state banks.[2] By contrast, the overwhelming majority of state firms were happy with their domestic sales and profitability and had little problem raising funds, so for those state firms, going global was an easy option.

This is the irony of China's success over the past decade. Even as the country raced up the global league tables, the state sector grew more powerful as it squeezed out private firms and turned back the clock on market reforms. In the autumn of 2011, I co-authored a report with KPMG looking at future multinationals in China, interviewing CEOs of big foreign firms across the country. "Suffocating" was the most common response when asked about state-owned competitors; what the foreign multinationals were saying in public, many local firms were saying in private.

And yet this is the China that the rest of the world has become accustomed to over the last ten years, contributing to the popular belief that China might one day rule the world, or at least the commercial world, as the country's powerful state firms storm abroad, acquiring resources and market share as a result of their cheap labor, cheap capital, government support, and vast economies of scale. The limited information on just how these companies strike deals and what level of government support they receive has only served to emphasize the mystique of the almighty Chinese state firm.

But that is about to change as China's economy runs up against major growth challenges and is forced to transition away from an investment-led model toward a consumption-driven one. It's a change that is already creating space for the country's leading private firms that are carving out niche opportunities.

The rise of the country's affluent middle class is among the most important of those opportunities. Why go abroad when China is home to one of the world's largest and fastest-growing consumer markets? Instead, a growing number of private firms are looking to acquire brands and technologies to bring home. Sure, the country's economic growth is slowing, but Chinese consumers are also maturing fast and demanding more choice and better quality. The more nimble private firms are responding to the development and, in doing so, changing China's commercial engagement with the rest of the world.

Just consider some of the recent transactions: Dalian Wanda, one of China's largest conglomerates, bought the American cinema operator AMC Entertainment in 2012 and then acquired the British yacht builder Sunseeker the following year; Fosun Pharma purchased a majority stake in the Israeli medical equipment company Alma Lasers in 2013; Shuanghui International Holdings, one of China's largest meat-processing companies, purchased the American pork producer Smithfield Foods also in 2013.

Wanda's acquisition of AMC best illustrates the upside. The Asia-Pacific cinema box office is growing fast and will shortly rank as the world's largest, overtaking that of America. And, in the Asia-Pacific market, China ranks number one. Indeed, in the first half of 2013, China built an additional 419 cinemas as ticket sales rose by $470 million.[3] So why not acquire a foreign cinema chain to transfer management expertise and technologies home to China? This is a different and arguably more persuasive story when compared to a Chinese construction firm winning contracts in Saudi Arabia or a Chinese railway equipment company looking at opportunities in Vietnam.

To be fair, the development shouldn't be a surprise: China is following the trajectory of other more developed markets, a point that is best illustrated by comparing China's top 100 nonfinancial multinational firms to those in the rest of the developing world. Not unexpectedly, China's list is heavily weighted toward companies in the resources or related sectors: the big oil companies, such as PetroChina, CNPC (China National Petroleum Corporation), and CNOOC (China National Offshore Oil Corporation), all rank high on the list, followed by chemical companies such as Sinochem, transport and storage companies such as China Merchants Group, and metals companies such as China Minmetals Corporation.

Now, these types of firms are also common in other emerging market countries, such as Malaysia's Petronas or Korea's POSCO. But what is still missing from China's list are the privately owned service-sector firms, such as Hong Kong's Shangri-La, a hotel company; Malaysia's Genting, a gaming company; India's Tata Consultancy Services, a consulting company; or South Africa's Naspers, a media company. If China is to follow the same trajectory as other developing and formerly developing markets, we can expect a transition away from faceless resource giants to companies like Wanda.

If such a transition occurs, this will require building more brands. So far, China has struggled to do so, partly owing to a ruthlessly competitive domestic sector and weak intellectual property rights protection. In the autumn of 2012, I was engaged on a study with the European Brands Council in Hong Kong; one common complaint among foreign brand owners was how Chinese manufacturers assumed that producing cheaper versions of a foreign design, as opposed to outright copies, was an acceptable business practice; in their eyes, they were innovating on price rather than style.

Recognizing this, the country's leading private firms have taken a shortcut by acquiring brands abroad to bring home. Eventually, these companies may well build out global businesses. But for now, they are more likely to behave as did today's American multinationals in the 1950s or 1960s and focus on a booming home market.

This in turn creates a new set of opportunities for foreign business owners looking to tap into China. Of course, multinationals are already striking deals and even selling businesses. However, smaller companies are also increasingly finding opportunities: some are cash-strapped firms looking to sell; others are hoping to find an equity partner who can grow their business in China. But, ultimately, the most successful are offering a brand or technology that adds value to a Chinese company in its home market and recognizing the needs of private firms and the more nimble state firms.

No doubt the largest Chinese state firms will continue to build out global businesses, and even grow them successfully. For instance, I have heard positive views on some Chinese oil companies in the Middle East. They don't provide the full spectrum of services. But in many areas they are world-class. This is not uncommon among state companies that are particularly good at a specific product or process where requirements for operating in the China market are higher than overseas, for instance on account of the country's unique climatic or geographic conditions, with the oil sector a good case in point.

Nevertheless, state firms are also facing a reality check as the favorable conditions that once nurtured their growth have soured. China's GDP growth rates have fallen by a third to near 8 percent, even as aggregate debt has reached 270 percent of GDP and is approaching American and European levels.[4] Not surprisingly, state banks are starting to worry about their nonperforming loans. The government is also beginning to push back, raising the share of profits that state firms are required to pay to the state and even investigating for corruption the head of the state agency responsible for the country's biggest 117 state firms.

That may result in a shakeout of mid-tier state companies that rushed abroad for the wrong reasons, such as political motivations.

"Officials might encourage a state firm to go abroad—sometimes for strategic reasons or sometimes just to generate publicity in the local media and make a lot of noise," said Tony Shi.[5]

We caught up again in the summer of 2013 after Shi had changed jobs and was free to speak more openly. I pushed him for more details on how those motivations might skew a state company's overseas business strategy. "We were always focused on the volume results and set lofty sales goals," he recalled. "But the sales department was scrambling to meet those goals and so we didn't pay attention to whether we could actually service the cars once we had sold them. I heard many complaints in Mexico, Russia, and South Africa about a lack of spare parts and services."

He continued, "The state firms also tend to prefer absolute control over any foreign partnership and so reap most of the benefits." I had heard similar criticism from other Chinese nationals and foreign executives who worked alongside the big state companies abroad. But as Shi argued, "You absolutely need a strong foreign partner in certain countries. Take the case of Foton in Russia, a country notorious for a murky and tough business environment. The company opted for a weak partner that we could control. But the partner doesn't have the *guangxi* [relations] to deal with the local government."

It was in Saudi Arabia that I found a snapshot of the challenges for these mid-tier firms. The country is a mixture of developed and developing. Wealthy Saudi industrial families are used to dealing with blue-chip brands such as Scania, Xerox, and Kimberly-Clark, as well as employing seasoned Arab, American, and European veterans to run their business. However, the country's appetite for building roads, railways, and sewers is similar to that in any developing country. The fact that American, European, Korean, Japanese, Indian, and Chinese firms freely compete also makes for a hypercompetitive market.

In the late 2000s, Chinese state firms appeared to be swamping their foreign competitors, some reportedly bidding at significant discounts and winning deals. I was visiting Riyadh several times a year pitching for projects and armed with a long list of Chinese success stories: China Civil Engineering Construction won a contract to build a railway between Riyadh and Qassim; Dongfang Electric Power Corporation was hired to build an independent power plant; Guangdong Overseas Construction Group was commissioned to construct new buildings at King Khalid University. All were evidence of these opportunities.

I was met with plenty of interest, but also often with the same qualification: "We are happy to speak with Chinese companies. But we want quality. Cheap labor and cheap products don't interest us. Show us the future world-class champions." I was stumped. Those future champions certainly exist, but not yet in large numbers.

Perhaps the concerns were exaggerated by popular stories about cheap Chinese electronic goods that broke shortly after they were bought or those that zapped the owner. But by 2012, anecdotal evidence was emerging that some Chinese firms were indeed running into challenges. The Saudi Education Ministry publicly claimed that its contract with Chinese construction firms was a "failure."[6] Meanwhile, the local press reported that some Chinese firms were pulling out of contracts after being asked to raise their quality to international standards. The firms agreed but then renegotiated their contracts and raised the price to a level similar to that of their American and European competitors.

It was similar allegations of quality that contributed to a $630 million loss for the China Railway Construction Company on its construction of a light railway between the holy cities of Mecca and Medina. The Chinese press claimed that the terms of the contract were changed as Saudi authorities, "more accustomed to Western standards," put in redesign requests related to station size and earthworks. The company responded by throwing staff at the politically important problem without consideration of cost, with one Chinese manager saying, "Tickets from Beijing to Saudi Arabia were in short supply for a while—the flights were full of people from China Railway."

What went wrong? Perhaps it was partly mismatched expectations. The Chinese firms were bidding at exceptionally low prices, and Saudi clients might have initially thought they were getting a bargain. But as Shi argues, "Yes, Chinese firms are cheaper because of their cheap labor and raw materials. But quality can suffer."

There were also other reasons. For a start, many of the firms simply weren't yet international enough. I dug into the background of around 50 Chinese companies with registered offices in Saudi Arabia and found that a third originated in China's less developed interior provinces where government relationships are crucial to winning contracts. That doesn't necessarily imply a lack of international capabilities, but it raises the risk that these firms aren't yet ready to work abroad; I recall Saudi contacts complaining at the time about the unwillingness of many Chinese firms to collaborate with local partners.

For these less mature firms, trying to find the right mixture of quality and price to compete against a seriously competitive mix of American, Korean, or Turkish contractors in a large and developed capital project market is a huge challenge. In fact, the results showed in 2013 when a series of firms bid for the prestigious Riyadh underground railway project; this was the same year that China was building subways in 18 cities at home. The three consortiums bidding for the project included a long list of American, European, Korean, Indian, and local firms. But no Chinese company joined the bid.

The performance of Chinese firms will vary widely between countries. Nevertheless, Saudi Arabia's unique mixture of developing and developed market conditions makes the country a useful lens into the world of Chinese state firms and suggests that the best performing will pull ahead even as others flag.

Ambassador Paul W. Speltz has been deeply involved in these changes over the past four decades, having first arrived in China in 1972 and building a successful consulting business in the country that he and his associates later sold to Citicorp. He was appointed by President George W. Bush as US Ambassador and Executive Director to the Asian Development Bank and, concurrently, the first US Treasury Envoy to China in 2002. After leaving office, he joined Kissinger Associates as President before finally setting up his Asia-focused advisory firm, Global Strategic Associates. Not surprisingly, having seen China transition from Mao suits to high-speed trains, he has some colorful stories to tell.[7]

One such story from the 1980s is a reminder of how fast China's engagement with the rest of the world has changed. Speltz recalls being asked by the then China National Instruments Import Export Corporation to purchase a small "suitcase size" portable computer on behalf of a local university. "The university was fascinated by them and literally cut out a 2-inch-by-2-inch article on the latest product called an 'Apple.' I was requested to purchase and bring back to China one 'sample' unit. So even though we thought the name Apple was rather silly, we agreed to help and I visited Steve Jobs's very small facility in California and purchased a couple of units over the next few months.

"Apple even asked us to help them establish sales in China. But we turned them down. Large computers were a very sensitive US-government–controlled product at the time and, besides, we felt that even if Apple were to receive clearances on a large scale, who would ever buy a product named after a fruit—Apple? What a mistake," Speltz says, shaking his head in mock regret.

I asked Speltz about the biggest change in China's current outbound activity. "It's these smaller Chinese companies that are doing so much better. The company's directors are more responsive than they used to be. They are more sensitive to local labor unions and politicians. Many have received Western educations or attended business schools." I asked about the state firms. "They are still moving very slowly. And still very much in the old manner. When we meet with them, many of the younger managers realize that they have to be more flexible. But institutionally these enterprises are still set in their ways."

The upshot is that China's commercial engagement with the rest of the world is evolving much like its own economy. I would expect that the best-performing state firms will continue to improve and will emerge as fierce competitors for the world's other multinationals. But the weaker performers will struggle, just as they have in Saudi Arabia, and will likely retreat to their home market. Most exciting, though, will be the rise of the country's leading private firms that have managed to wrestle some opportunities away from the state sector and are now looking to add value to their businesses by bringing the best the world has to offer back to China.

WANG WANGPING WAS EATING BREAKFAST AT HIS FACILITY IN THE EASTERN Libyan port of Tubruq when he took the call. His manager reported that thugs had razed a nearby Turkish facility to the ground, and it was at that point that Wang started to worry. Rightly so. He was an engineer for a Chinese construction company, and the date was February 18, 2011, shortly before Libyan protestors took control of the streets of the eastern city of Benghazi.[8] Wang tried to calm his wife by SMS as she watched from China while events unfolded. "It's nothing. Everything is good," he recalled saying when later speaking with reporters from Xinhua, China's state news agency.

But he wasn't being entirely honest. Wang was worried and was already taking emergency precautions. He ordered his senior management to collect passports and increase the number of guards on duty. He then spoke with his staff and advised everyone to pack and get ready to move.

On February 19, his walkie-talkie crackled to life. "There are some armed thugs outside," he was told. Wang told all his staff members to bring their bags and meet at an agreed-upon location. He then walked out to meet with the Libyans and negotiate. "We are targeting Gaddafi, not Chinese people," the thugs reassured him. But even so, some had been drinking, and they grabbed cash and mobile phones from the staff. Wang and his colleagues decided to flee the building the next day. They were just in time; their construction site was robbed the same day by armed men who stripped the place bare, taking trucks, cranes, loading equipment, and computers.

Two days later, Wang and his colleagues managed to hire 11 minivans with the help of staff from the Chinese embassy in Cairo. It took the group of 85 Chinese nationals over 11 hours to get through the land crossing into Egypt, but they finally made it, much to the relief of Wang's tearful wife, who had watched the crisis worsen on television.

China's evacuation of 36,000 nationals from Libya was the largest such evacuation in China's history and a warning of risks ahead. China's commercial push into Libya was seen as a sign of the country's growing commercial strength, and with good reason, as the country's firms won dozens of construction contracts. By the second half of 2013, the last year data were made available by the Ministry of Commerce, there were 871,000 Chinese laborers working overseas, with the largest share likely working for state firms.[9] Yet, the figure is probably multiples higher when thousands of undocumented workers are included.

To put it another way, imagine if there were 871,000 Americans building railways in Libya, selling clothes in Egypt, or laying cable lines in Afghanistan, many operating largely unprotected. How would that impact America's engagement with the rest of the world, especially the developing world?

Just as China's outbound commercial activities are starting to follow the trajectory of other countries, so might the country's political and security relations. Of course, for its part, China tends to emphasize commercial relationships rather than political ones. I recall a conversation with a Xinhua journalist working in the Middle East who said, "We are often asked to avoid politics entirely. Just focus on the economics." But that may be increasingly difficult to do as stronger commercial engagement with the rest of the world tests China's policy of nonintervention in the political affairs of another country.

The events in Libya are only one demonstration of the risks. In this instance, Chinese firms and nationals simply got caught up in a major political event. However, in other cases, Chinese nationals have been more deliberately targeted as a result of their commercial activities. Take the killing of 13 Chinese nationals on the Mekong River in northern Thailand in October 2011. The incident involved an ethnic Burmese drug lord and corrupt Thai antinarcotic police forces. The killings sparked popular anger in China, although it was never clear whether the sailors were set up or were involved in drug trafficking.

Chinese nationals are also occasionally targeted as a result of China's growing commercial and political prominence. Take the events of July 2009 after majority Han Chinese and minority Uyghur Chinese clashed violently in Kashgar, a city in the western province of Xinjiang. Muslim leaders largely overlooked the clashes with the exception of Turkish Prime Minister Recep Tayyip Erdogan, who sided with the Uyghur partly because of their Turkic roots. However, Islamic

Maghreb, the North African branch of Al Qaeda, threatened to retaliate against Chinese workers based in Algeria.

Had China finally caught the attention of the global Islamic groups? So far, the country had largely appeared to escape the attention of Al Qaeda and its affiliates as extremists instead focused their attention on America and Europe, as well as on other countries involved in the 2003 invasion of Iraq.

I first heard about the threat in Hong Kong in late July 2009 while having a drink with a contact at a global risk consultancy. One of his colleagues and a specialist in extremist groups had discovered the threat in an Arabic-language chat room popular among Islamic extremist groups. The consultancy, with an office in Hong Kong and strong connections in China, had apparently alerted the Chinese Foreign Ministry. They heard nothing more and assumed that the ministry had either ignored the warning or preferred to deal with it internally rather than open a dialogue with a foreign firm.

Hong Kong's *South China Morning Post* broke the story a few days later, and the report ranked as one of Google's most widely read stories globally, with the Chinese press also reporting the incident and linking it to events in Xinjiang. Shortly thereafter, the Chinese embassy in Algeria posted a Chinese-language warning on its website, advising Chinese nationals in the country to guard against attack. I was struck that the warning made an explicit connection between the events in Xinjiang and the risk of retaliation in Algeria rather than trying to deny a relationship between the two.

However, local factors were also at work. There are an estimated 32,000 Chinese workers in Algeria, mainly building apartments, roads, schools, and public offices. Not all leave the country when their contracts end, and a number have set up stalls in the country's capital, selling cheap goods imported from home. In August 2009, clashes broke out between Chinese and Algerian youth in the city's Bab Ezzouar district over a parking dispute.[10] Shortly afterward, the government tightened visa restrictions when rumors spread among a panicking population that a wave of 150,000 foreign workers was about to arrive.

Events in Algeria illustrate how local grudges have a nasty way of combining with global politics, and China's growing commercial presence around the world and its increasing political clout suggest that these incidents are more likely to grow in number over the coming years, much as they would for any major power.

Indeed, the recent American experience aptly demonstrates how single individuals can influence a country's foreign policy and its international reputation. Consider how Japanese anger was inflamed in October 2012 after two US sailors were accused of raping a young woman on the island of Okinawa, the site of a major US military base; or the outrage when a US soldier killed 16 Afghan civilians in March 2012. Military personnel overseas are not the only source of problems: when an American pastor burned a copy of the Quran at his church in Florida in March 2011, riots and deaths in Afghanistan resulted.

The political and security challenges of operating in so many challenging markets may yet reshape China's commercial engagement with the East and the rest of the developing world, just as the country's private firms are changing the pattern and purpose of outbound investment.

In traveling between Asia and the Middle East, I am often struck by the disconnect between local clients and big Chinese companies. Many local professionals talk of finding it tough to reach out to their counterparts or to understand their motivations. There are exceptions, of course, but relying on cheap labor, cheap debt, government relationships, and, in some instances, corruption, has allowed some Chinese companies to operate in a bubble. Certainly many are reluctant to hire the lawyers, lobbyists, and public relations teams that can help smooth a foreign company's entry into a new market.

These challenges aren't limited to Chinese companies. Nevertheless, China's commercial engagement with the East and the rest of the world appears to be exiting its honeymoon period as the novelty wears off, and that will require companies to adapt much as competitors from the rest of the world have done.

Security risks are just the hard edge of the change. But there are also more subtle political challenges. In Vietnam, where tensions over the South China Sea have clouded the business environment for Chinese companies, some might find investment approvals harder to obtain in the event of worsening relations. Or consider Saudi Arabia, where China's "noninterventionist" stance on Syria is seen as "interventionist" by many of the country's Sunni-majority population. These aren't issues that have thus far disrupted business, but they may sway a commercial decision against Chinese companies.

Nevertheless, China's security relations with the East and the rest of the developing world are already evolving, in spite of the country's "noninterventionist" stance, and are among the stronger signals that we are entering a new period—and a more complicated period—for Chinese companies.

So far, there have been some easy fixes for the country's security challenges, such as relying on local security forces to protect Chinese assets or simply paying off local armed groups. However, local security forces are often of poor quality and can't be relied upon during a major incident, especially in the event of a hostage situation. Events in Libya and Algeria demonstrated that simply throwing money at the problem is not always possible if the conflict is either too broad or too deep rooted. These are quick fixes that may have worked when China faced only limited security challenges.

There may be a better template, especially for those situations where the country doesn't have permission to dispatch its military even for evacuation efforts and understandably wants to avoid the sight of People's Liberation Army special forces fast-roping into hot spots against the wishes of the sovereign power. That example is the American military's use of private security forces in Iraq and Afghanistan: in early 2009 there were almost 190,000 American troops in the two countries, but also another 20,000 private security contractors and 260,000 private general contractors.[11]

Might China similarly use private security forces to defend its interests? It would certainly help avoid a direct confrontation between sovereign powers. I raised the question with a number of academics around 2008, and many felt "uncomfortable" with the idea. It didn't fit comfortably with a policy of "nonintervention."

Yet, in late 2011, the State Council did just this, introducing a law permitting private Chinese security companies to send their staff overseas. Shortly thereafter, Shandong Huawei Security Group opened the country's first foreign private security service. The company had a 20-year history of providing domestic security services. Many of its staff were former People's Liberation Army veterans, and they provided a wide range of services from security surveillance to armed guards. The company claimed domestic clients such as China Tobacco and Sinopec, as well as strategic alliances with foreign security firms.

In a 2011 article, Wang Yuelin, a security expert at the People's Public Security University in Beijing, and Wang Ying, a legal expert at Guangzhou University, summed up some of the key challenges, arguing that China's rights were being "gobbled up" and that the problems had worsened in recent years, whether because of terrorism, social unrest, or the global financial crisis and resulting joblessness. The authors argued that much as China had privatized its own economy, it should privatize its overseas public security, as might any major power, and that the country's already flourishing domestic security industry and large numbers of retired soldiers and police would assist the transformation.[12]

Those retired soldiers were certainly key, and one Chinese contact familiar with the industry made the point to me privately in 2013 that the government encouraged the security companies to hire ex-special forces if only "to keep track of them once they left the military, rather than have them fall into crime."

In February 2012 there were suggestions that those private security contractors were already at work in Sudan after the Sudan People's Liberation Movement-North took 29 Chinese workers hostage. The *Wall Street Journal* later reported that a dozen armed private Chinese security contractors had joined Sudanese troops involved in the rescue, citing Sudanese military officials. Chinese media reports on the rescue either failed to confirm any Chinese involvement or simply repeated verbatim the original *Wall Street Journal* article, suggesting official sensitivity toward the subject back home.[13]

If Chinese private security contractors were involved, it wouldn't be a surprise, as Chinese companies were also already hiring foreign security companies. While serving as US Ambassador and Executive Director to the Asian Development Bank during the early 2000s, Paul Speltz was spending much of his time in Afghanistan, Pakistan, and neighboring countries.

"Part of my role was to reach out to other countries and have them help Afghanistan's development, loaning money, providing technical assistance, even building roads and bridges. China was initially very slow coming in on that side because of their concerns on security. They had a very bad incident where they were working on a road project in the northeast and quite a few of their laborers were slaughtered in their tents. The Afghans said it was robbers, but it was an anti-foreign operation, possibly because not enough protection money was being paid to tribal leaders in that area. They learnt the hard way," he says.[14]

So how did they respond? "They ended up hiring US private contractors. They ended up paying some of the same private security firms that we were using and they went forward with the project."

The country's big test then is the huge Aynak copper mine about 25 miles southeast of Kabul, which has a daily production estimated to be eventually worth over one percent of the global total. The China Metallurgical Group won a 30-year lease to operate the firm in 2007, but what happens when the American military pulls out? The firm appears to already have considerable protection using three rings of security: the outer ring is Afghani and the middle ring is foreign. The inner ring, however, is Chinese. After an American withdrawal, the firm might want to consider strengthening those rings. But which one?

If foreign security contractors are already selling their services to Chinese companies, it would not be surprising if Chinese security companies soon followed in larger numbers, whether because of their ties to the big Chinese state companies, the lower cost of their services, or the value put on confidentiality.

Security challenges may also more specifically motivate firms to enter joint ventures or hire a larger number of locals. For the typical multinational, foreign employees account for more than half of the total employees.[15] Few Chinese companies could match those figures. But for companies operating in Egypt, for instance, how might they respond to the fact that 25 Chinese nationals were recently kidnapped by disgruntled Bedouins in Egypt's Sinai Peninsula? Perhaps it is better to employ locals? It would certainly make for good domestic politics in a country where unemployment rates are skyrocketing.

The upshot is that China's commercial engagement with the East and the rest of the world is in flux as a result of the country's growing economic and political clout. That is neither good nor bad, but it suggests that change is inevitable, especially for those firms that have operated in a bubble until now.

CHINA'S GLOBAL RISE HAS CAUGHT ATTENTION OVER THE PAST DECADE partly because it seemed so exceptional. It appeared that Beijing was directing from the commanding heights as the country's state firms locked up resources and undercut foreign competitors. It even had a slogan, *Go Global*, just to ram the point home.

Are we witnessing the end of that exceptionalism? The fact that privately owned companies such as Dalian Wanda are now leading the charge suggests that China's global rise is following a similar trajectory to that of other emerging countries; these firms are making acquisitions in nontraditional sectors, especially services, and are buying for commercial reasons. Understandably, many of these acquisitions are made in America and Europe as these companies are looking to acquire technologies that might benefit the core business back in China, where growth opportunities are often large.

If the change is sustained, then it is a positive development. Rather than big state companies looking to acquire large tracts of farmland, for instance, more nimble private firms may look to buy stakes in food-processing companies, a less politically charged act, especially for Western governments worried about popular backlash, and one that creates local jobs and exports. It is also a more value-added activity that taps into China's increasingly affluent consumers, especially in the West where agricultural productivity is already high but where there is limited understanding of how best to market processed products in China.

At the same time, I would expect to hear a divergence opening up between the leading Chinese state firms that are emerging as truly competitive multinationals, such as Sinopec, China State Engineering

Company, or Sinochem, and those mid-tier state firms that are strug-gling to build on their initial overseas expansion. Should China's leadership decide to genuinely squeeze the state sector, through a com-bination of financial reform, slower growth, and regulatory reform, the country's mid-tier state firms may have fewer resources or less interest to expand abroad.

The case for China's private security companies is less straightfor-ward and still in its early stages. However, the country's security chal-lenges have certainly grown in recent years even as the world expects more from China as a global economic and political power. This doesn't imply an end to China's policy of nonintervention, but it does argue for a blurring of the lines and better protection of Chinese commercial interests abroad by Chinese security companies. Such a policy change is likely to grab headlines, and yet China would simply be behaving much like any other global power, and its firms responding like any worried multinational.

The benefits to service providers are potentially large, and not just for private security contractors. The typical Chinese company is still hesitant to engage professional services firms such as lawyers, lobbyists, or public relations when operating overseas. In part, this is because such activities are not especially important to winning deals in China. But they are becoming increasingly important abroad as China's grow-ing clout means that the dividing line between business and politics is blurred more frequently, and more attention is paid by disgruntled locals to foreign companies using graft to win business.

Security and political challenges in the East may also prompt more Chinese companies to look to the West. For now, many companies are finding it easier to grow their market share in the less developed markets in the East and the rest of the developing world. However, the opportunities in America and Europe are clearly significant, especially as Chinese firms start selling a higher-quality product, one for which they have applied successfully for intellectual property rights protection in their target countries. In this case, the relatively stable markets in the West will grow in attraction.

The implication is that China's global rise might start to normalize, following the trajectory of other countries, not just those in America or Europe, but also countries in the developing world, such as South Africa and Turkey. Of course, the fact that China's economy is larger than those of Brazil, Russia, and India combined means that the scale of these purchases will inevitably attract more attention from the international media and foreign politicians alike. But a qualitative shift in that investment should be welcomed, especially if it implies the rise of a more robust Chinese private sector.

6

SMALL TRUCKS AND
BIG PLANES

TRANSPORT AND LOGISTICS
IN THE NEW EAST

F OR A PERIOD, HONG KONG'S CONTAINER PORT WAS THE LARGEST IN
the world, intermediating much of China's trade with the rest of
the world during the 1990s. The port's history dates back to 1972
when the first vessel, the *Tokyo Bay*, arrived at the newly completed
docks. The asphalt at Terminal One had only just been laid, and there
were worries that the *Tokyo Bay*'s 200 containers would stick to the
quayside. They didn't, and after a devastating typhoon knocked out the
region's main container facility at Kaohsiung port in southern Taiwan,
Hong Kong's new port was soon booming.[1]

For a visitor to Hong Kong, the port is easy to spot when traveling
by train from the airport or flying in over the city at night, its bright

lights a complement to the lights of Hong Kong's financial district only a short distance away. Containers are stacked high, making the most of the port's small parcel of land, which is squeezed between the harbor and the industrial and residential estates on the other side of the main highway. Trucks shuttle between the port and mainland China, usually dropping off containers full of consumer goods before picking up empties.

But there's a problem. Hong Kong's container port might look busy, but activity has in fact stalled, and throughput volumes in 2012 were almost unchanged from their level five years earlier. That's a major change from the boom years between 1990 and 2005 when volumes grew at a brisk 10 percent clip annually, except for a dip during the Asian financial crisis. Part of the decline is explained by the rapid growth of competing ports in the neighboring Chinese cities of Shenzhen and Guangzhou. Together with Hong Kong, these cities claim three of the world's ten largest ports.

Even so, there are other influences at work, and the challenges for Hong Kong's container port can be explained by a historic change in the way the region does business.

For much of the past few decades, the East was mainly shipping goods to the West, whether Asian consumer goods to America or Middle Eastern oil to Europe. The region's share of global trade rose steadily during the period, from 18 percent in 1990 to 36 percent in 2012. So powerful was the region's rise that it doomed one of the world's historic trading corridors, the Transatlantic, as trade between America and Europe peaked as a share of global trade during the last two decades and has fallen steadily since.[2] Today, it is trade across the Pacific Ocean and through the Suez Canal that matters.

The legacy of the East's rise is easy to spot. The region accounts for 15 of the world's top 20 container ports—Shanghai, Singapore,

Hong Kong, Shenzhen, Busan, Guangzhou, and Dubai, to name a few. It is also home to most of the world's biggest port operators—Hong Kong's Hutchison Port Holdings, China's COSCO, Singapore's PSA International, and Dubai's DP World, all of which operate ports at home and abroad. Over the past 20 years, the East has risen to rule the waves, ending centuries of dominance by the West since the arrival of the first European trading ships in Asia during the 1500s.

But that's only the beginning. What happens next promises to be an even greater change. Whereas the East once traded principally with the West, it is now turning inward to serve local markets. Undoubtedly, sending goods by sea will remain a dominant form of transport, but road and rail are increasingly important channels for transporting products to local consumers. And that's a problem for Hong Kong's container port. The port benefited from free-spending Americans and Europeans, but what happens when it is the Chinese who are buying—and they are spending principally on Chinese goods?

Indeed, the rise of China's inland provinces promises to be one of this century's most fascinating commercial stories. The inland provinces have a population of 720 million and a GDP worth $3,600 billion, meaning that they are more populated than Latin America (585 million) with an economy twice the size of that of Sub-Saharan Africa ($1,300 billion). Yet, over 200 major Chinese cities with populations greater than 750,000 lie some 150 miles inland from the coast. In effect, we are observing the rise of the world's largest landlocked economy, and that will change the way China looks at the world. From Guangzhou's factories to Shanghai's bankers, all are starting to look inward, rather than outward.

Symbolic of the change is Hon Hai's decision to relocate half of its nearly one-million-person workforce from Shenzhen to the inland cities of Chengdu, Wuhan, and Zhengzhou, more than 300 miles from the nearest coast. The Taiwanese company is the world's largest contract electronics manufacturer, producing most of the world's iPhones and iPads. Its decision was partly in response to labor shortages and rising costs in the coastal provinces. But it also underscores a shift in economic gravity and the resulting jobs and income growth in the inland regions.

Easily overlooked, but equally important is the rise of mainland Southeast Asia, a region that includes Cambodia, Laos, Malaysia, Thailand, Vietnam, and also Singapore, given its land bridge to the mainland. The region is only modestly smaller than China's inland provinces with a population of 620 million and a GDP of $2,300 billion. Moreover, the emergence of Vietnam in the 1990s and of Myanmar more recently, together with the move toward an economic union in 2015, a group known as the ASEAN Economic Community (AEC), are all powerful forces for the rise of another major inland economy.

For now, the growth of road and rail transport is mainly due to trade within, rather than between, countries as local manufacturers and retailers respond to stronger domestic demand. But gradually cross-border trade between countries will also strengthen. And for all the attention paid to China's large inland regions, it is Thailand that best characterizes this development. Not only is the country's inland demand flourishing, but Thailand is also strategically located at the heart of mainland Southeast Asia and so is well positioned to benefit from a rise in cross-border trade.

AFTER ARRIVING IN BANGKOK, MOST TOURISTS QUICKLY TURN SOUTH toward the beaches. Yet, most of the country's inland population is found upcountry. Some 36 million people live north of Bangkok in

Thailand's many regional villages, towns, and cities that are spread across a wide geography of mountains and river deltas.

Khon Kaen is typical of those cities. Home to 110,000 people, it is a regional hub for surrounding farming communities, many living in towns of just a few thousand. The city's central districts are a mix of hotels, government offices, and small shops. Of course, compared to Bangkok's massive urban sprawl and 15 million inhabitants, Khon Kaen might appear more like a small rural town, but its strategic position in the country's northeast makes it one of three main centers for a regional population of 21 million people, and the city itself is only a short 125-mile drive to the Laotian capital, Vientiane, to the north.

Indeed, for all the attention paid to Bangkok's packed shopping malls, it is in Khon Kaen and other regional cities where a consumer boom is emerging that is changing the way the country's retail and logistics sectors operate as they start to pay attention to opportunities outside the country's huge capital.

Angkana Songvejkasem is Linfox's General Manager for Thailand and has been a close observer of the changes in the country during her 15 years at the firm, having seen Thailand emerge from the ashes of the financial crisis in the late 1990s to the more recent growth of inland demand. The Australian logistics company is one of the country's largest foreign players with over 3,500 employees and 900 vehicles, serving local and multinational clients ranging from Tesco Lotus to Unilever. When we met in 2013, Songvejkasem had just returned from meeting with industry peers to talk about efficiency in the grocery sector and supply-chain costs.

Songvejkasem was quick to remark on how fast the industry was adapting. "The retailers are driving the change. They are developing a smaller store format due to a shift in consumer trends as well as city planning regulations," she says.[3]

"But that changes the way we deliver. The smaller-format stores don't have much storage room, so we need to deliver two to three times a week. We used to supply the stores directly from our Bangkok distribution center using large trucks. But now we need to use smaller trucks to improve our costs and speed of response. Many companies, both retail and fast-moving consumer goods [FMCG], are building new logistics hubs in the major cities of each region, such as Khon Kaen in the northeast, Lampang in the north, and Surat Thani in the south, where we can consolidate and distribute to these smaller trucks."

There is a large six-foot-tall map of Thailand on the wall of Linfox's meeting room with the country's road network marked out in detail. We walk across so Songvejkasem can point out the changes taking place upcountry. "You wouldn't believe what's happening in Khon Kaen. It's in a strategic position to capture cross-border trade between Cambodia, Laos, Vietnam, and Myanmar. Land prices have jumped between three and five times in the past few years, especially around the ring road where land was cheap. The local government is also spending on roads, railways, and bridges," she says.

"I've also seen more high-rise condominiums and traffic jams recently," adds Songvejkasem, a remark that is usually a good indicator of development in Asia. It's also not bad for a town that once made its money mainly from farming, and it might even convince the city's natives working in Bangkok to return home.

The development in Thailand's northern regions illustrates the transformational change taking place across the rest of mainland Southeast Asia. The rise of the consumer means more people spending in more cities, but also more people spending in smaller and more inland cities. Whereas it was once possible for local and foreign retailers to operate large superstores in just a few cities, they are now operating smaller stores, in larger numbers, and across more locations. Logistics chains are increasingly complicated as a result, as goods are shipped to regional distribution centers and then reloaded onto smaller trucks.

Yet the opportunities for a company such as Linfox are difficult to ignore, in spite of the challenges. Linfox's Asia operations are today larger than its operations in Australia as the company grows its business not only in Thailand, but also in Indonesia, Singapore, and Vietnam, primarily targeting blue-chip foreign multinationals.[4] The growing complexity of supplying local consumers offers opportunities for mid-sized logistics firms able to provide innovative solutions, not just as a result of rising inland demand, but also as shoppers buy more goods through online stores or marketplaces.

The opportunities are still primarily focused on shipping goods within countries. But Khon Kaen's development also demonstrates the potential changes in the region's logistics industry as the Southeast Asian countries move closer to forming an economic bloc. The ASEAN Economic Community (AEC) will connect 270 million people by land, if measuring just mainland members, and a total of 620 million by land and sea. Even if the community remains challenged by non-tariff trade barriers or corruption at borders, it will nevertheless be a powerful growth cocktail for trade between countries.

China is not part of the AEC, but the country's sheer size and the fact that it shares a border with Laos, Myanmar, and Vietnam also make it a possible regional game-changer as trade between mainland Southeast Asia and China's southern and southwestern provinces continues to strengthen and road and rail links improve.

If ties do strengthen, then the southern Chinese city of Kunming, situated just 185 miles from the Vietnamese border town of Lao Cai, will serve as an important hub for the region. The city receives 15 daily flights from Southeast Asia and is the launching point for a future high-speed train linking up with China's southern neighbors. Kunming isn't large by Chinese standards, with a GDP of $40 billion and a population of 3.4 million. However, the city's strategic positioning is crucial as it enjoys easy access to Laos, Myanmar, and Thailand via a road network that, at least on the China side of the border, is relatively robust.

It is the potential tie-up between China's inland provinces and the inland economies of mainland Southeast Asia that is especially exciting, as it creates a regional economy that is significantly larger than that of most other emerging markets, in terms of either population or output. The impact on cities such as Kunming or Khon Kaen will be significant—indeed, it already is, judging by the amount of construction taking place as both cities look to the future. The development may be slower than some hope, but just as the world's center of economic gravity is drifting east, so it is moving inland.

NEVERTHELESS, THE RISE OF INLAND TRADE WILL NOT BE SMOOTH. IN ASIA, it is often said that it is easier to ship goods to consumers overseas than to those at home. Factories are usually located near ports, which are often built and operated by some of the world's largest port operators. Once goods are loaded on ships, it is a straight run to their final destination in Los Angeles or Rotterdam. But as the region's domestic demand strengthens, supply chains will inevitably become more complex because goods shipped inside a country are more vulnerable to a host of challenges, from poor roads to traffic jams to natural disasters.

And just as Thailand is a good study of what happens when it goes right, it also illustrates what can go wrong. Craig Hope-Johnstone is now DHL Supply Chain's Head of Operations for South and Southeast Asia, but in late 2011, he was DHL Supply Chain's Managing Director for Thailand and watched as his business vanished beneath historic flooding.

I had arrived at Hope-Johnstone's office 15 minutes early, having misjudged the city's snarling traffic and enjoyed a surprisingly clear run from the Asok BTS station. Bangkok is one of the few cities where expense receipts can read: *subway, light rail, taxi, and motorbike,* anything to ensure that you arrive on time for a meeting, or at least within a 30-minute range. Having started his career in Australia, Hope-Johnstone has lived in Thailand for the past six years and can provide colorful accounts of Bangkok's traffic. But I am in his offices to hear about those ten weeks in 2011 when it was Hope-Johnstone's job to help make sure that the city didn't run out of food.

"The government approached us during the first two weeks of the flooding, after most of the grocery warehouses went under. They were obviously concerned no groceries were getting to the retail outlets and the population was having major issues finding enough food and water," he recalls. "The Deputy Prime Minister asked to set up a cross-stock warehouse in 72 hours to stock products for retailers and we were offered 100,000 square meters [about one million square feet] of free warehousing near Don Mueang airport," referring to Bangkok's second airport, used primarily for budget airlines and located around an hour's drive northeast of the city center.[5]

"The problem was much of it didn't even have roofs and was unusable. We managed to find 15,000 square meters [about 161,000 square feet]. Even this had some problems with infrastructure, but we hired local electricians and roofers to make repairs," he says. Hope-Johnstone also faced other, more political problems. Local bureaucrats had parked their cars in the warehouse to avoid damage from the floods. Officials weren't the only ones worried about their cars: locals who didn't have access to the warehouse had triple-parked on highway overpasses, making it difficult for DHL's trucks to even reach the warehouse.

But eventually, with a large team on site, the company managed to start shipping groceries in and out of the warehouse within the 72-hour deadline set by the government. Bangkok could breathe easy again as supplies of bottled water, rice, and other consumables started to reach the capital's grocery stores.

But then the Don Mueang area itself started to flood. Worried about rising floodwaters, Hope-Johnstone had suspended operations shortly before the water started rising. Officials were reassuring the population that the area was safe at the time, but Hope-Johnstone and high-ranking air force officials were less certain. "I told my team we would relook at the situation the next morning and then make a decision." By the next morning, the government's flood crisis agency itself had packed up and left Don Mueang, where it had been temporarily based.

Less than a week later, the government offered DHL another site. "At that point, it was getting bad. The water manufacturers had all gone underwater. There were no eggs or noodles. And they were starting to have to import supplies from Malaysia. The government offered us a site in Rayong, south of Bangkok, which had been earlier repossessed for unpaid taxes, and where they had three large buildings that were empty," he recalls. Again, DHL had the site operating within 72 hours of the government's reconnecting the power, and the site dispatched groceries for the next six weeks.

So how do you protect against floods in the future? "The problem is you can't," Hope-Johnstone replies. "Factories can put their transformers up on blocks or build defensive walls around the facility. That prevents damage to the factory equipment itself. But it still doesn't mean you can ship goods from the factory if the roads are flooded." I ask if there is a solution. "Personally, I can't see it," says Hope-Johnstone. "Look, even Phahonyothin Road was flooded. This was built back in the 1930s and was billed as protection for a once-in-a-100-year flood. But the road was completely submerged during the height of the floods."

That suggests long-term implications for Thailand: given its importance to the global automotive and electronics component parts industry, there were certainly worries at the time that manufacturers would leave the country altogether. Hope-Johnstone is more sanguine on this particular risk. "Sure, the car industry was hit badly. Honda lost 1,000 cars to the floods. But many of the parts manufacturers and smaller component manufacturers have simply moved south where the floods didn't reach, rather than leave Thailand altogether."

However, he doesn't discount the potential damage from future floods. "There are two reasons," he says. "First, this wasn't just a short-term disruption. The floods were here for a long time. Second, the transport industry itself was badly impacted as people were driving through water and trucks were getting damaged—engines, gearboxes, etc. There's no middle tier in the transport industry, and the lower-tier players don't invest for the long term so they have older equipment and are vulnerable to flood damage."

Thailand's experience underscores the challenges of shipping by road rather than by sea. Of course, seas don't flood. And while the scale of the flood in Thailand might have been historic, floods themselves are not. In fact, during 2012 and 2013, the list of Asian cities that found themselves flooded was impressively long: Beijing (population 15 million), Wuhan (9 million), Kunming (3 million), Jakarta (10 million), and Manila (12 million). These floods prevented logistics providers from supplying local retail stores for days in the worst-affected areas and even for weeks in cities where the floodwaters were slow to subside.

Moreover, floods aren't the only threat. Earthquakes, landslides, and typhoons are regular threats in the region and can disrupt inland transport for significant periods of time. Typhoons and heavy storms regularly shut down activity in southern China for 24 hours or more. Earthquakes in southwestern China can cause road blockages, and landslides in Malaysia are a common occurrence. If volcanoes might appear to be an obscure threat, I recall being diverted in 2007 by the Sidoarjo mud volcano that continued in 2013 to disrupt traffic traveling south from the Indonesian city of Surabaya.

The sad reality is that Asia is more vulnerable to natural disasters than any other region in the world. The United Nations has attempted to quantify the risks, measuring the number of cities vulnerable to a disaster including flood, cyclone, drought, earthquake, landslide, and volcano. There are nearly 100 cities worldwide at "high risk" from two or more of these hazards and, critically, 74 of those cities are in the East. The region already accounts for half the world's population, but it also accounts for two-thirds of the world's cities at high risk from a natural disaster, with obvious implications for supply chains.

The upshot is that the rise of the East's inland trade is driving major changes in the region's logistics sector, whether as a result of having to supply smaller stores and rely on redistribution centers, or to protect supply chains against natural hazards and potential disruptions to the smooth flow of goods within a country.

Colin Airdrie has seen the best and the worst of the region's supply chains over the past 35 years. Currently the Managing Director of Logistics Bureau Asia, a specialist logistics consultancy, he was formerly the Head of Regional Development for IDS Logistics, the third-party logistics arm of Li & Fung, a Hong Kong–based global sourcing firm, as well as Senior Director of Logistics for CR Vanguard, one of China's largest retail chains. Together, Airdrie's two former employers supply a sizeable share of the goods sold to consumers in America and Europe and, increasingly, to shoppers in China.

Today Airdrie is based in Bangkok, and he has seen the rise of Thailand's inland trade firsthand. "It's the development of modern trade that drives an efficient logistics network. This is the sector that has the highest levels of customer service, rapid turnover of inventory, tight purchasing and delivery procedures, and on-shelf availability. In other words, an effective end-to-end supply chain. The modern trade retailers would die without this," he says. "If the total supply chain practice is poor, then no amount of good infrastructure can get things working at their optimum level."[6]

The need to support the development of more efficient supply chains in the East will in turn create commercial opportunities for those foreign companies able to import best practices and technologies from abroad, applying the experiences learned from helping the West develop its own modern retail trade business.

CHUNGKING MANSIONS IN HONG KONG'S TSIM SHA TSUI DISTRICT IS notorious for its flophouses with their 50-square-foot hotel rooms catering to backpackers and traders. It is also home to some great Indian and Pakistani restaurants and the only decent place in Hong Kong where I can find the full range of genuine Bollywood movies. Walk into the building, and you feel as if you are transported to Chennai, Karachi, or, increasingly, Lagos, for the number of African traders visible in Chungking Mansions has grown steadily in the past decade, alongside China's economic rise.

Yared Desta is one of those traders. I meet him late on a Friday afternoon in the spring of 2013 at an African-owned store on the building's second floor offering an eclectic mix of logistics and other services to new arrivals. He is from Ethiopia and is in town for just a few days before crossing the border to mainland China.

"Cheap goods," he says. "That's what I'm here to buy. I have a small store back home where I sell them."[7] It's not an uncommon story.

In fact, there are even more African traders living across the border itself, mainly in Guangzhou, where they fill some of the city's bigger churches on a Sunday. Indeed, the number of African traders visiting China has risen fivefold in the past decade from near 100,000 to over 500,000 by 2012 as the country's export factories produced just the type of affordable clothing, footwear, and household appliances suited to Africa's growing consumer markets.

Traders like Desta are critical to the region's commerce as they buy for their own stalls or shops. And the African, eastern European, or Latin American traders staying temporarily at Hong Kong's Chungking Mansions are just a sample. In my previous book, *The New Silk Road*, I wrote about the Chinese coastal city of Yiwu and its 200,000 Arab traders who visit the city's vast exhibition halls to stock up on goods each year. But there are also compelling stories to be written about the Africans who fill Guangzhou's churches on a Sunday, or the 5,000 Indian textile traders who live in Keqiao, not far from Yiwu.[8]

It's not only traders. Talk to most bankers, lawyers, or other professionals in the region and you'll learn that they probably spend much of their time on a plane, shuttling between cities and countries. Phone calls and video links just aren't enough in a region where personal relationships are so critical to getting business done. My own story is similar to many others in the region: a typical year might include regular flights to more than a dozen cities, including Beijing, Kuala Lumpur, Mumbai, Dubai, and Cairo, and all the gaps in between. Sadly, airports become as familiar as home.

That's good news for the region's airlines. If land transport is one beneficiary of the region's growing demand, air transport is another. The East might not yet dominate the world's air traffic as it has shaped its sea-lanes, but it is quickly catching up. The region accounts for five of the world's top ten airports by international passenger traffic—Hong Kong,

Dubai, Singapore, Bangkok, and Seoul. It is also home to some of the world's largest airlines—Emirates Airlines, Cathay Pacific, Singapore Airlines, as well as more recent arrivals such as China Eastern Airlines and China Southern Airlines.

This is especially good news for Hong Kong. Even as the city's ports have struggled for business, Hong Kong International Airport has not. Passenger arrivals have risen over 50 percent since 2005 with more than 20 million people from other countries in the East arriving each year. In response, Emirates Airlines, Korean Air, and Singapore Airlines have each added an extra 5,000 weekly seats on their flights to Hong Kong in response to that increase in demand, even as British Airways, Lufthansa, and Continental Airlines have seen their own capacity stagnate or even fall sharply.

It is traders such as Desta who contribute to the gains at Hong Kong's airport. But Hong Kong isn't even the region's biggest story. I asked each of those African traders at Chungking Mansions how they flew to Hong Kong. Some flew on Ethiopian Airlines and others on Kenya Airways. But the most common response? Emirates.

IN 2008, TERMINAL 1 AT DUBAI INTERNATIONAL AIRPORT WAS DEFINITELY feeling cramped. Passenger traffic had grown rapidly in the previous years, and the airport was full of people: British tourists standing jet-lagged in duty-free stores, Pakistani workers trying to catch some sleep on the floor, and African traders holding large carry-on bags full of sample merchandise. By the spring of 2009, Dubai had fully opened the airport's new Terminal 3, a vast complex with 26 gates and the capacity for 40 million passengers a year. I arrived on an Emirates flight at 1:00 a.m., expecting the terminal to be empty.

It wasn't. It was jammed full of people and looked no different from Hong Kong's Tsim Sha Tsui underground station at 9:00 a.m. on a

Monday, except on a much bigger scale. Originally hoping for a seat in a café, I ended up going straight to the gate to avoid the crowds congregating in the terminal's central area.

In 2013, Dubai subsequently added a new concourse to Terminal 3, purpose built for the huge Airbus A380s, and further raising the airport's total capacity to 75 million passengers per year. Not content with that, the emirate is also building a new airport, Dubai World Central, to the southwest near the Jebel Ali Free Zone. The airport is designed to eventually receive a stunning 160 million passengers a year. However, the project's initial phases are focused on developing Dubai World Central as an aviation logistics hub with three times the air-cargo capacity of Hong Kong International Airport, already the world's busiest airport by cargo traffic.

That might appear ambitious given Dubai's credit problems during the recent global financial crisis, but it's all a question of scale. For all that Dubai captures media headlines, the emirate's economy is still relatively small when compared to the East's giants. After all, Dubai's $80 billion economy and population of 2 million is small compared to Beijing ($280 billion economy and 15 million population); yet, zoom out a little and Beijing appears small when compared to China ($8,200 billion and 1,300 million). Zoom out again and China accounts for less than half of the East ($18,000 billion and 4,200 million).

Those numbers work in Dubai's favor. Just a small uptick in trade or passenger traffic between Asia and the Middle East can mean a huge relative gain for Dubai's transport sector, not to mention the spillover benefits to the tourism and business services sectors. So long as Asia grows, then so should Dubai.

And it's not just trade between Asia and the Middle East that matters: the bigger prize is Africa. Dubai sits as a convenient midway point for Asian traders and companies looking to do business on the continent. Take a look at any map and draw a line from Beijing to Lagos—the line inevitably crosses through Dubai. And that's only for those able to travel in a straight line between the two cities. More often the only choice is to transit through Dubai via Emirates, or fly Abu Dhabi's Etihad Airways or Qatar's Qatar Airways, two increasingly fierce competitors for passenger traffic between Asia, the Middle East, and Africa.

The rise of China's e-commerce trade also suggests that Dubai might benefit from even stronger express freight business as a hub for goods shipped to shoppers buying online in the Middle East or Africa. The emirate's duty-free status and large industrial parks might equally serve as regional warehouses for Chinese online retailers.

Indeed, Dubai offers Asian companies an attractive business hub, especially for those dealing with North and East Africa, where the populations are often Muslim, speak an Arabic dialect, and have strong historical ties to Dubai or the Middle East. For instance, in spite of all the talk about China's growing trade with "Africa," some 26 percent of its total trade with the continent was with North Africa in 2012. Whereas some multinationals might base this business out of London, there is a good case for Chinese firms to use Dubai for the same purpose, rather than setting up multiple branches in often less secure and less business-friendly cities.

For now, Chinese firms are only just expanding their global networks. But my conversations with Chinese banks and securities firms in both Hong Kong and Dubai suggest that those banks with operations in Dubai have experienced a sudden increase in activity and staff numbers. In the autumn of 2012, for instance, one of China's larger banks was already rapidly expanding its operations. "They are bringing in a whole crew, some 35 people, including Arabic speakers," said a contact familiar with the situation, describing how the bank had taken out a large space at the Dubai International Financial Centre in preparation.

In the 1970s, Pan Am, an early American airline, was still operating two daily around-the-world flights stopping in Honolulu, Bangkok, Delhi, Beirut, Istanbul, Frankfurt, and London. It was a long-haul crawl as Pan Am 001 flew westward from San Francisco and Pan Am 002 flew eastward from New York.[9]

Much has changed since then, and while there are other stories in the region that underscore the importance of air travel, Dubai's role as a transport hub stands out as it illustrates the importance of connectivity to the region's rise: African traders traveling to China, Indonesian pilgrims flying to Saudi Arabia, Pakistani workers heading off to the UAE, and Kuwaiti tourists vacationing in Malaysia are all critical to the region's commercial growth. And unlike Pan Am 001 or 002, Dubai is helping people fly from north to south, not only east to west, making the emirate central to the region's rise.

IF PASSENGER TRAFFIC IS CRITICAL TO THE REGION'S RISE, ITS DISRUPTION is also a disaster. Events in 2013 offered a personal lesson in the vulnerabilities of the region's air industry. At the time, I was shuttling between China and the Middle East, and I watched keenly as viruses broke out in both parts of the world.

In late March, the Chinese health authorities confirmed three cases of human infection with avian influenza, or H7N9. The first case was an 87-year-old male in Shanghai who died just 13 days after he first started coughing up phlegm. As the virus spread, officials shut down all of Shanghai's live poultry markets, believing that the flu was spread through direct contact with infected fowl. TV news programs led with scenes of health officials wearing protective white suits, plastic boots, and masks disposing of the poultry, with over 20,000 chickens, ducks, geese, and pigeons killed in the Huhuai agricultural market in the city's southeastern districts.

The economic impact was immediate, with sales at KFC stores falling 16 percent during March and international airlines suffering a 7 percent fall in share prices during the period as worries grew that this latest virus would be a repeat of the deadly SARS virus in 2003 that killed 774 people in 11 countries, including 349 people in China.

My wife was understandably paying close attention to the events during the time, given that her brother and his wife lived in Shanghai, while I was on a flight almost every week. We made a trip to a pharmacy in Hong Kong's central district to buy high-quality masks to send to her brother, just in case. By the time we left, three others were in the shop stocking up. New infections eased by late May at around 130, and the disruption to travel was limited. I recall flying on an empty plane to Taipei during the peak of the SARS crisis in 2003, but events in 2013 were far less dramatic with planes full as usual.

China did not have a monopoly on viruses that year. In Saudi Arabia, the country was already dealing with a different virus that had a significantly higher casualty rate; whereas birds were the source of H7N9, camels were appropriately linked to the Middle East respiratory syndrome (MERS).

The MERS virus was first identified by an Egyptian virologist in December 2012 and was a strain similar to the SARS virus. Infected patients had also turned up in London. Fortunately, the virus spread slowly, and a World Health Organization emergency panel of experts determined in July 2013 that the virus was not at the time an emergency threat to public health. Indeed, most of the over 90 cases were restricted to Saudi Arabia. But with death rates running at nearly 50 percent, there was understandable concern that the virus might spread through the region's busy airports.

Those concerns were fueled by the fact that 3 million Muslims from 180 countries attend the hajj in Mecca each year, an event lasting six days. It is the largest gathering of people in the same place for such a short period anywhere in the world. Most are traveling from the East; rough estimates suggest that 60 percent arrive from other Arab countries and another 30 percent from Asia. Of those, nearly 90 percent arrive by air, and on arrival often sleep in close quarters, such as in the enormous tent cities at Mina during the second day. In short, the hajj has always faced major health hazards from the mass transmission of disease or virus.

The hajj was scheduled for October 2013, and events in Shanghai were still fresh in the minds of many. Indeed, the Chinese State Administrator for Religious Affairs warned of the risks, appealing to Chinese pilgrims to take care and citing the Quran in its alert.[10] Recognizing the risks, the Saudi government also warned in 2013 that it would not issue hajj permits to the elderly or to those with chronic diseases in order to prevent the spread of the virus. The number of pilgrims was later cut by 20 percent that year owing to expansion work at the Grand Mosque, a fortunate coincidence.

The twin outbreaks were a timely warning that the East is vulnerable to pandemics whether because many of the world's viruses originate in China or because the number of international passengers traveling through Dubai, Hong Kong, and Singapore each year is more than twice the number traveling through Heathrow.

Flu prevention has improved since the SARS outbreak, and most Asian airports are equipped with temperature detectors. Hong Kong still regularly conducts checks. Emergency response plans have also improved, judging by the speed with which Chinese authorities both reported the initial outbreak and subsequently shut down the city's live poultry markets, winning plaudits from the international medical community. The Director General of the World Health Organization also publicly noted China's more rapid and transparent sharing of data with international bodies and institutes combating the virus.

But the economic impact can still be significant. Hong Kong's airline passenger traffic offers a good illustration of the impact. In 2002, shortly before the SARS virus struck, passenger arrivals to Hong Kong averaged around 1.4 million a month. But by April 2003, the number had dropped dramatically to just 420,000 before falling again in May to 280,000. The international airlines were quick to respond and cut capacity aggressively; the number of flights landing at Hong Kong International Airport halved from around 9,000 arrivals a week to just 4,500 during the period. For an international hub such as Hong Kong, the effect on business was a disaster.

Trying to measure the overall impact of a virus, however, is a thankless task. Some companies can operate remotely even as others struggle, and I recall sourcing agents and Hong Kong–based factory owners struggled to inspect their mainland factories regularly. It was much the same for bankers and lawyers who need to conduct due diligence on a company's operations. The impact on the domestic services sector was even greater, with hotel occupancy running at just 17 percent during the worst of the crisis and restaurants often empty, especially in the city's business districts. Many small businesses took years to recover from the financial hit.

Just consider the impact on Dubai from a similar crisis. Even during the worst of the global financial crisis, hotel occupancies never fell far below 70 percent in 2009, judging from public and private data.[11] International arrivals slowed during the period, but only turned negative for a few months. In effect, if Dubai were struck by a virus on a level similar to SARS, the effect would be many multiples greater than that of the global financial crisis on the emirate's services sector. For a city shuttling people between Asia and the Middle East, these are serious risks, as they are for the rest of the region's logistics hubs.

Hotels might struggle to fill rooms and airplanes might fly with empty seats, but other businesses have options, especially in an era of tablet computers and cloud computing. The region's vulnerability to travel disruptions should be a spur to the type of software and equipment that allows employees to work remotely and productively, staying in contact with clients and colleagues. And where direct contact is critical to daily operations, the outsourcing of due-diligence work or factory inspections is only likely to grow in demand, especially among those foreign companies without a local office.

In an era when the East's airports function far more effectively than do many in the West, it is tempting to overlook the need for such business contingency plans. But the events in 2013 were a timely reminder that the region's complexity and importance to the global economy is multiples greater than it was ten years ago during the SARS crisis.

THE RISE OF THE EAST AS A MARKET FOR ITS OWN GOODS WILL BE A SOURCE of both strain and innovation for the region's logistics networks. And if container ships characterized the region's rise over the past two decades, trucks and aircraft more appropriately describe the next two decades as domestic markets continue to expand.

Local companies are in a position to benefit from that change. The region's airlines already enjoy strong growth as local hubs are protected from excessive foreign competition. Moving goods between countries by sea, such as between Thailand and Europe, is also much easier than within a country by road where protectionism and other practices can challenge foreign competitors. Local trucking firms, for instance, can use their deep relationships to good advantage and may also be prepared to pay off officials to overload trucks or avoid inspections, an option unavailable to most foreign firms.

Foreign logistics providers are nevertheless in a better position to deal with the growing complexities of supplying local demand. For instance, Hong Kong–based Kerry Asia Road Transport, one of the region's largest logistics companies, introduced a less-than-truckload service between China and Vietnam in the winter of 2012. The twice-weekly route between Shenzhen and Hanoi was intended to offer a similar transit time as air freight but at a lower rate. This is the type of niche service that local competitors will struggle to offer, but it is critical, especially as the region's e-commerce business booms.

The challenge for foreign companies will be deciding how to most efficiently serve inland regions, rather than just the big spenders in major cities. The importance of third-party logistics providers will grow as companies outsource their supply-chain management to firms providing operations, warehouse, and transportation services. Logistics firms may even try to muscle in on the retail business itself. SF Express, one of China's largest logistics companies, is already growing an online grocery business through its subsidiary SF Best and making good use of the parent company's logistics infrastructure.

The opportunities are also not limited to shipping goods or people for business. The region is increasingly going on vacation. Southeast Asian governments have allowed budget airlines to flourish, rather than protecting incumbents, after recognizing the value to tourism. Today, the region has more than 40 budget airlines, and the number of visitors to Southeast Asia from North Asia, South Asia, and the Middle East has risen by 9 million in the past decade. North Asia has also enjoyed similar gains, and on a trip to the village of Shirakawa-go on Japan's west coast, I heard as much Mandarin, Korean, and Thai spoken as Japanese.

Worries about a pandemic persist, especially for those of us who fly regularly. And the potential economic repercussions are significant for a region that seems ill suited to conducting business virtually. Relationships are still critical to getting business done and demand regular travel. For those firms that have invested in business contingency plans and developed strong local offices or robust relationships with local suppliers, the ability to get on with business will help to not only maintain market share, but even capture share should the disruptions be prolonged.

7

THE EAST'S UNCERTAIN URBAN FUTURE

TARGETING THE REGION'S FAST-GROWING CITIES

THE TYPICAL CHOW TAI FOOK STORE LOOKS EXPENSIVE, AND IT should, as some of the jewelry and watches for sale are worth more than a year's income for the average shopper. The company's name is written in white characters across a rich red sign, signifying good fortune, outside each store, and attentive staff stands inside behind brightly lit display boxes. There are the standard silver wedding rings and gold necklaces found in any high-end store worldwide, most featuring a single or multiple diamonds, as well as a wide collection of jade bracelets and gold animals depicting the Chinese zodiac.

That description would be familiar to almost any Chinese national; the Hong Kong–based jewelry chain has 1,708 stores in

259 cities across China. In fact, Chow Tai Fook has a larger operation than Tiffany & Co., the American jewelry multinational, even before counting the company's stores in Hong Kong, Taiwan, and Macau.

But then, Chow Tai Fook has benefited from China's rapid urbanization over the past decade and from the country's huge number of cities. Of those 1,708 stores, more than half are located in cities with a population greater than 750,000, similar to Boston or Leeds. Chow Tai Fook is a reminder that when we talk about commercial opportunities in China, we are talking about the country's hundreds of lesser-known cities that will be a major source of revenue growth for the rest of the world for many years to come, long after saturation of the usual list that includes Beijing, Shanghai, Guangzhou, and Shenzhen.

And if Chow Tai Fook is looking to expand to the rest of the region, there is plenty of scope for growth. Already, the firm has stores in Hong Kong, Taiwan, Malaysia, and Singapore, targeting mainly ethnic Chinese shoppers. But how about India, Indonesia, or Korea? It might mean acquiring local brands or a new product offering, but the opportunities are surely tempting as these three countries have 86 cities each with a population greater than 750,000. The sheer scale of the company's existing operations, as well as its potential for future growth, is a reminder that the East's rise is taking place on a scale unlike that seen in the West over the past century.

In the 1960s, New York, London, Paris, and Moscow were still the world's most populated cities and, with the exception of Moscow, the most prosperous. Indeed, the East accounted for only nine of the world's 30 largest cities at the time. But during the next 40 years, the balance of power shifted steadily eastward. By 2010, the East accounted for 16 of the world's 30 largest cities: Delhi, Mumbai, Kolkata, Beijing, and Shanghai were just some of the region's new urban giants, as their rapid economic growth gradually shifted the world's center of economic gravity from West to East.

The projections are equally mind blowing. The United Nations Population Division estimates that the East's urban population is expected to rise by an additional 1.5 billion people by 2050, a figure equivalent to nearly one-half of today's global urban population.[1] China and India account for the largest gains, but equally significant shifts are under way in Indonesia, Pakistan, and the Philippines.

These are the sorts of figures that can easily impress. A few snappy PowerPoint charts can tell an exciting story about vast commercial opportunities, and rising purchasing power or high birthrates among existing urban households are only the beginning. Equally important is the fact that the region's urban population is projected to grow by a massive 50 percent over the next 40 years as a result of migration from villages and towns. That's potentially an extra 50 percent of urban consumers needing more banks, more restaurants, and more supermarkets among a range of goods and services. Heady times indeed.

It's not only the sheer size of the East's urban population, but also the number of cities, that makes the story so different from what we have seen over the past century. In 2010, the East had 325 mid- and large-sized cities with a population greater than 750,000. By contrast, there were just 134 similar-sized cities in the West, mainly found in Europe and the United States. The East's big cities such as Guangzhou, Jakarta, Mumbai, and Riyadh usually catch attention, but it's the less obvious locations such as Hefei, Surabaya, Jeddah, and Chennai that matter equally and are often overlooked.

And it is China that captures the challenges with 143 mid- and large-sized cities with populations greater than 750,000. For all the focus on Beijing, Shanghai, and Guangzhou, those three big cities together account for just 6 percent of China's urban population. The real opportunities lie in the country's less well-known cities.

The Home Inn in the western city of Xian is one example of those opportunities. The room has a frugal look with its laminate floors and a simple bed. There is a small heater, and free tea and coffee are provided. But there are no toiletries in the bathroom, just a container of liquid soap attached to the shower wall. The hotel resembles a converted office building from the outside. But then it should, as Home Inn is one of China's rapidly expanding budget hotel chains that occupy converted hotels and office buildings across the country, offering a simple but standard room at a very reasonable price.

"The budget hotels are for the masses. But they are especially popular among traveling sales representatives, or 'road warriors,' who have a per diem of around 200 yuan a day," says Ernst Zimmermann.[2] A 30-year resident of Hong Kong, Zimmermann opened Beijing's first foreign hotel, the Lido, in 1983, and has either established or been involved in over 70 hotels across the country. "In the past, those salesmen used to get together, two or three to a room, and rent a 5-star hotel rather than stay in a 3-star. But the budget hotels have changed all that, offering a decent alternative for a single salesman."

I periodically catch up with Zimmermann for business, and we ate at the Hong Kong Club in the autumn of 2012. He recalls opening an Ibis hotel in Chengdu, in western Sichuan province, in 2004. A year later there were local copies all over the city. Zimmermann asked his local manager how many, to which he received the reply, "About 300."

The budget hotels have enjoyed spectacular growth in the past five years as they respond to the expansion of the country's mid- and large-sized cities, especially in the inland regions. The hotels were originally clustered in three parts of the country—the southern Pearl River Delta, the central Yangtze River Delta, and the northern Beijing-Tianjin corridor. But the global financial crisis called for a change of strategy as these regions were hit hard by the slump in demand. So the budget hotels started expanding in the central and western provinces, opening in such inland cities as Changsha and Zhengzhou.

Today, Home Inn has more than 1,900 hotels in over 200 cities: Baoji, Tieling, Weinan, and Yiyang are just some of the smaller and lesser-known locations. Chow Tai Fook might represent spending by the affluent or those well-connected individuals making good money from government spending. But Home Inn and its road warriors are symbolic of a more everyday rise in spending as corporate salesmen travel across the country, much as their American counterparts did in the 1950s and 1960s, trying to get their products into retail stores and businesses.

The challenge for any foreign company then is where to start. Some companies, like British electronics retailer Dyson, have the financial muscle and commercial motivation to build multiple outlets across multiple cities. But smaller companies do not and so will benefit from a more selective strategy.

Critically, local companies face the same set of challenges. Take the budget hotel industry. Home Inn might have a relatively even spread of hotels across the country, but its competitors do not. Motel 168, for instance, is almost exclusively concentrated around Shanghai and the Yangtze River Delta. So is GreenTree Inn, albeit with stronger representation in Beijing and the Bohai Rim area. The latter two companies have concentrated their efforts in markets where they have stronger relationships and deeper insights, much as the early Western hotel chains did.

Focusing activities on a collection of cities grouped in a tight geography then makes sense, especially in China, where the sheer number of mid- to large-sized cities means there are a number of important city clusters across the country, some as large as individual economies in the East, and even in the West.

Take the city cluster centered on the southern coastal city of Guangzhou. Here, Home Inn has 113 hotels in 10 cities. Together these cities have a GDP worth $680 billion, or more than that of Switzerland, and a combined population of over 40 million people, so there is good reason for the budget hotel chain to zero in on the thousands of road warriors looking to target this region. This also makes the city cluster an ideal candidate for a foreign company looking to tap into China's urban consumers without the risk of draining resources by opening up stores in multiple cities in far-flung parts of the country.

The city cluster also benefits from a rapidly expanding mass-transit system that will connect all 40 million people within one-hour's travel time. The 35-minute ride from Guangzhou's city center to the neighboring city of Foshan is already turning the latter into a dormitory city. The trains are new and comfortable, looking little different from those in Europe. Not everyone I speak with is prepared to travel so far, but Guangzhou is gradually conforming to life in a typical Western city, and long commutes may be inevitable for households looking for cheaper or larger places to live.

Jump on Guangzhou's rapidly expanding underground, and a 40-minute ride also takes you to the enormous Chimelong Safari Park in the southern suburbs where the new, and increasingly affluent, Guangzhou is on display. Giraffes and zebras roam freely, and white panthers stare at families during breakfast as young children press their faces to the other side of the thankfully thick glass. Nearby is the spectacular Chimelong International Circus with its Chinese and eastern European acrobats, performing seven days a week to packed audiences paying $40 a ticket, an indication of a flourishing services sector.

Further south again and Hong Kong's Fok family is developing an 8.5-square-mile region in the southern district of Nansha. The privately funded development has reclaimed huge amounts of land and built roads, ports, and other infrastructure to support what will eventually be one of southern China's most desirable regions. It even includes a marina designed and built to European standards to serve the burgeoning demand for yachts and motorboats. The area's Matsu temple is a highlight, recently refurbished using tens of thousands of kiln-dried bricks reclaimed from Guangzhou's older buildings that didn't survive the city's development.

Opportunities abound in the region: providing services to the growing number of families moving out to Foshan; offering leisure and entertainment options for hardworking families looking to relax over the weekend; or selling high-end lifestyles to the ultrawealthy as they pull their boats into the Foks' marina.

And yet the success of Guangzhou and its neighboring cities will not be straightforward to copy: not all Chinese cities enjoy the same resources, and many suffer from bad policy making. The experience of the American industrial city of Detroit is a cautionary tale for China, especially for those cities and city clusters that are overly reliant on activity in a single sector, such as construction. In the 1960s, Detroit was a shining example of all that was great about America. Today, roughly one-fifth of the city's housing stock lies either abandoned or blighted, and the population has shrunk by more than half.

The topic of China's debt is worth a book by itself. But, in short, local governments found themselves strapped for cash over the past decade and therefore used bank loans and special-purpose vehicles, among other channels, to raise significant amounts of debt worth at least $1.75 trillion, or 27 percent of GDP, to fund spending on roads, metros, and concert halls, among a range of items.[3] Some of the spending was worthwhile, some of it was not. Take a drive around Guangzhou and its neighboring cities, and it's hard to spot excessive construction. But in other parts of the country, the white-elephant projects loom large.

Consider Zhuji, in coastal Zhejiang province, where the city is building vast numbers of residential apartments around a third beltway in imitation of Beijing. The problem is that the existing city limits of this largely rural market town don't extend far beyond the first loop. Meanwhile, Zhuji's gleaming new financial district was largely empty and only partly finished when I visited in the autumn of 2011, not surprising for what is only a small regional city. But that has not stopped officials from pushing ahead as they forecast that the city's population will rise by 150,000 to 500,000 in ten years.

Not everyone agrees. Indeed, one of the country's top urban planners, Li Tie, said about Zhuji, "It's not right to say bigger is better. Bigger just means more problems." And Zhuji had certainly stored up some problems for itself as the government, worried about rising debt, started to turn off the credit taps.

Or take Changde in inland Hunan province, where the city is in the process of building an international marathon track around the picturesque Liuye Lake. The track was already two years into construction when I visited in the winter of 2011, but it was little more than sticky red mud that clumped to the bottom of my shoes. I stood beneath a blue metal board advertising the track's location with little to see but discarded steel drums. Not far from the area were the familiar sites of half-finished residential apartment buildings and multilane roads passing through empty tracks of land.

To be fair, Changde has a better chance than Zhuji of growing without a lifeline of cheap debt. The city has allocated some of the spending to develop the lake as a tourist attraction, and some of the facilities are certainly impressive. Nevertheless, this largely agricultural city was still building too much, too fast.

Indeed, as China's trend growth rates slow, it will be harder to sustain such growth. During the 1990s, China suffered from overinvestment in its manufacturing sector with the result that prices of clothing and household appliances fell steadily in subsequent years. During the early 2000s, the country spent mainly on infrastructure and property. In the case of Guangzhou's mass transit, that spending made sense. But it makes less sense for Zhuji as the city tries to fill its half-finished apartments, or for Changde as it tries to pay the bill for its international marathon track. These mistakes can place a drag on growth.

The experience of Zhuji and Changde underscores that not all cities are equal and that as China's economy slows, foreign companies will need to be selective in their exposure. The idea that all mid- and large-sized cities are good growth stories will be tested as those municipalities that have spent poorly will be left with unproductive infrastructure and few sources of sustainable growth. Chow Tai Fook might have a store in Changde, but there is no Home Inn. And a city more able to spend on high-end jewelry than on a decent budget hotel points to an economy that is poorly balanced and at risk of slowing.

And yet, slower growth might also create niche opportunities. The problem for local governments is that cities aren't cheap to run. Farmers largely look after themselves. But once they migrate to cities, they need their garbage collected and their children educated. For the most part, municipal governments across China, and much of the East, typically avoid the problem by distinguishing between formal and informal urban residents: formal residents have access to public services, whereas informal residents are often denied local residency registration rights and so instead have to pay out additional fees to private suppliers.

This raises the question of whether cash-strapped cities will be more willing to allow private companies to step in where the government can't. Certainly a user-pays system is increasingly attractive in the West where local municipalities have faced budget pressures. Sanitation is usually a popular place to start as private companies collect commercial and household garbage. Education is another, and while China has plenty of private kindergartens or after-school education centers or cram schools, the state still accounts for the largest share of primary and secondary education.

Indeed, China appears to be developing both the American and European models of private versus public provision of services. For instance, for all that China is expanding its own European-style national health coverage, foreign-owned clinics and hospitals are a fast-growing business led by a mix of American, Japanese, and Singaporean firms. Much the same can be argued about the private pension industry, with China adopting a mixture of both the American and European systems, creating opportunities for private asset managers to manage pension funds for the country's middle class.

The upshot is that China's rapidly changing economy requires far more nuanced strategies as growth divergences widen between cities and city clusters. The country's leading regions, such as the city cluster around Guangzhou, will continue to offer sizeable commercial opportunities. But the idea that growth through urbanization will buoy all parts of the country is no longer true as China's debt-funding expansion reaches its limits. That means filtering out those cities that are vulnerable to a slowdown as the country's state planners and regulators curb unjustified local government spending.

In this instance, city clusters offer a hedge: Zhuji and Changde are both part of larger, more flourishing regions, albeit regions with very different growth drivers. And even if one city in the cluster fails, others may succeed. Fortunately, China offers plenty of choices, as no other country, not even India, offers companies the same number of cities or the same concentration of cities in an economy that now ranks as the world's second largest, meaning a regional strategy makes increasing sense, and CEOs and business owners are more likely to be asking, "What part of China?" not "Are you in China?"

EVEN IF SOME OF CHINA'S CITIES STRUGGLE, MANY, SUCH AS GUANGZHOU and its near neighbors, will remain good places to do business. Those cities especially benefit from robust infrastructure that allows consumers to travel smoothly, a modern retail trade that offers a range of products and prices, and, most unusually, tight restrictions on urban migration, meaning few slums.

It is a different story in many of the East's 182 other mid- and large-sized cities. Indeed, while the rise of the region's urban population appears compelling in a presentation, there is a real risk that, if mismanaged, rising urban populations will simply produce households stuck in poverty and unable to buy the type of everyday goods such as processed foods or toiletries that can boost sales for fast-moving consumer goods companies. Turning urban migrants into sustainable urban consumers is critical if the region is to benefit from its expanding cities.

Mumbai is a pinup for the East's urban challenges, with over 40 percent of the population living in slums.[4] To be fair, slums aren't easily defined, and while some are characteristic of the shantytowns shown in the Oscar-winning film *Slumdog Millionaire*, others are made of concrete breeze block, have running water and power, and are home to office workers. Trying to properly house this population is not only a moral decision, but also a commercial one, as households often find themselves paying excessive rents for poor-quality accommodation.

The Mumbai-based Society for the Promotion of Area Resource Centres, or SPARC, is working to fix that problem. Housed in a former British-era school, SPARC's offices aren't easy to find, and I check my email for directions upon arriving: the lane adjoining the Alankar Cinema to the left; between the Patel Ice Cream Shop and the Globe Restaurant; second building on the left. The big stone building is imposing but was left to ruin over the years and now lies in an industrial area where men move thick steel wires on wooden handcarts, and large black ravens attracted by bags of rubbish lurk on rooftops.

But that's reassuring when visiting SPARC, as the organization's mandate is to provide housing for some of Mumbai's 9 million slum dwellers,[5] not to look after its own comforts. And it's more reassuring hearing their story sitting around a shaky wooden table, rather than perched on a Herman Miller–produced Aeron office chair.

The sheer size of Mumbai's slums makes the city's Slum Rehabilitation Scheme worth paying attention to. Introduced in 1997, the scheme provides slum dwellers with title to their land and the right to power and water. Property developers are then permitted to negotiate with residents to develop their land in return for keeping a share for private sale, while also providing the residents with free apartments. On paper, the slum rehabilitation scheme sounds ideal. Property developers are incentivized to build housing for slum dwellers; the slum dwellers get properly built apartments; and Mumbai ends up with a smart-looking district.

Why aren't politicians then encouraging the faster redevelopment of slums if only to win votes? After all, and at least in theory, a slum dweller's vote *should* be equal to that of Anil Ambani, one of the city's wealthiest industrialists. This isn't China, where an official is more worried about Beijing's opinion.

"They get it. But they don't know how to go about it," says Aseena Viccajee, one of SPARC's senior staff.[6] "It's tough trying to coordinate the slum dwellers, property developers, and government agencies. It might make sense on paper, but bringing all the parties together is incredibly challenging." It is a crucial point. The best ideas often die because of the sheer complexity of bringing together all the right partners. And it's not a problem that is limited to India; it is a challenge for any country that is urbanizing rapidly and having to coordinate flourishing household, corporate, and government interests.

"The slum dwellers trust us. We've worked alongside them for years. But the developers just try and buy the residents off," says Viccajee. "The problem is the developers have conned too many slum dwellers over the years, and so the residents don't trust the developers anymore. That's why we have to get involved, as intermediaries." I ask about the banks and get a similar answer. "The banks want to get involved in financing slum rehabilitation, but again they just don't know how to go about it. It needs a community-driven approach." And that's not easy for a banker more accustomed to a corporate environment.

There's also the problem of resettlement. "We try to ensure that slum dwellers are relocated no more than one train station away from their place of work," says Viccajee. Slums are often tightly knit communities, a reason why many people don't leave even after finding stable employment. If slum dwellers are simply relocated to another part of the city, they might be disconnected from their communities and, in a city such as Mumbai, which is so poorly served by public transport, having to commute long distances can be expensive. Some slum dwellers simply return to their original slums.

If there is a striking difference from China's rapid urbanization, it is the role of community. Local Chinese governments, at least until recently, haven't had to worry about community engagement and have simply bulldozed older districts; robust growth has also provided more job opportunities and stronger income growth.

But it's too early to write off Mumbai's slums and the others across the East, from Bangkok to Jakarta to Manila. If the region fails to settle its new urban migrants, learning how to sell to slum dwellers and the urban poor will be critical to tapping into the region's growing cities, at least outside of China. Learning how to work alongside local communities will also be important: otherwise, local and foreign companies alike will find themselves trapped in pockets of affluence, such as Andheri or Mulund in Mumbai, but struggling to sell to the city's larger population.

My visit to SPARC reminded me of a trip some 12 months earlier to Cairo's slums. I was collected from my hotel on the banks of the Nile River by Hany el Miniawy, who kindly agreed to meet on a Saturday. He should have been resting after a long week, but I discovered that el Miniawy isn't a man who rests. He is an architect, but more importantly a social activist who spent his early career building sustainable homes for Algerian families. We drove quickly through Cairo, enjoying the luxury of empty roads on our way to the city's slum areas, which have expanded relentlessly over the past six decades.

In the local Arabic dialect, the slum settlements are called the *ashwa'iyyat*, or informal area; unlike the one-story shacks common to the slums in Mumbai, the settlements in Cairo are built of a standard red brick as high as five to seven stories tall and housing over 60 percent of the population.[7]

We arrived at Manshiyat Naser, one of the city's more famous *ashwa'iyyat*. El Miniawy's car bumped over a disused railway track as we entered the slum itself and drove into an alleyway that barely separated the tall red-brick buildings on either side. Our car squeezed past pedestrians who brushed up against the windows as we were forced to jockey around oncoming cars, finding space to maneuver even when it shouldn't have been possible. We stopped occasionally as el Miniawy greeted old friends, slapping his open hand into the palm of another man and greeting him with a gusty *"azayak."*

What is so striking about Manshiyat Naser is the sense of community. Sure, many are poor. But shops line the street, apartments are above, and familiar faces are everywhere. The slums work in spite of being ignored by the government, with family and friends providing what the government cannot.

I asked el Miniawy if there are any community banks nearby. "Banks?" he asked in reply. "They aren't interested in coming to the *ashwa'iyyat."* I could appreciate why, given the cost of rolling out a retail network. And yet, the idea that some two-thirds of the city's population is underserved seems like a missed opportunity. Much as Mumbai's banks are ready, if struggling, to provide mortgage financing to slum rehabilitation schemes, the potential for banking Cairo's urban poor also seems like a commercial prospect even if it's a harder challenge than serving the country's more affluent communities.

Building scale and a sustainable business doesn't necessarily mean targeting everyone living in slums. There are plenty of relatively affluent households with stable incomes and a strong attachment to their communities despite the physical drawbacks slums may present. Mumbai's more affluent slum residents, for instance, enjoy relatively regular electricity supply and commonly have television sets, air conditioning, and a range of household appliances. Consumption of processed foods, such as noodles and biscuits, is also strong. The sheer number of people living in slum areas makes even this small segment a worthwhile commercial opportunity for many multinationals.

These aren't new commercial strategies. However, given the forecasted 1.4 billion increase in the East's urban population over the

coming three decades, such strategies are likely to become more important should local governments struggle to turn their new urban arrivals
into urban consumers. Not every government can create a flourishing city cluster such as the cities surrounding Guangzhou. Indeed, the
potential increase in the size of the East's urban poor may even fuel
more innovative strategies, especially those that recognize the importance of community.

Take KB Fairprice, an Indian retail chain of small-format stores
stocking a range of essential items. The stores were set up by Kishore
Biyani, the CEO of Future Group, one of India's largest retailers.
Biyani recognized that Mumbai's urban poor felt intimidated by the
city's big shopping malls and preferred to shop locally. He deliberately
located KB Fairprice stores in local communities and the chain has
since expanded to 176 stores in what the firm describes as densely
populated urban areas, echoing SPARC's own community-driven
approach.

Or consider the mobile banking industry, as customers use their
phones to conduct transactions at "branchless stores," depositing money
in accounts stored on their phones and sending or receiving money by
SMS.[8] Indeed, some developing markets are leapfrogging developed
economies in this technology as they target the large number of customers without formal bank accounts.[9] The mobile health industry is
also a potential source of opportunity, as mobile health workers are
able to conduct basic health tests using portable e-health kits and then
deliver the results by phone, especially as smartphone adoption rates
rise among the more affluent urban poor.

IT'S HARD TO FOCUS WHEN YOU NEED TO SANDBAG YOUR APARTMENT. MY OLD
friend and former colleague Mike Every was looking tired on the other
end of a Skype call. I was pressing him on some commercial issues in

Southeast Asia, but he really didn't have the heart for it, and understandably so.[10]

It was the autumn of 2011 and floodwaters were creeping toward Bangkok's city center, having already inundated much of the country. For his sins, Every was the head of the building's tenants association. For the most part, that included dealing with slow-paying tenants, changes in wage rulings, and broken equipment. What he didn't expect was that the job would include sourcing sandbags to protect the building from rising floodwaters, all the while deciding whether to evacuate and flee to a hotel in one of the few parts of the country not flooded.

"There aren't sandbags in the city for love or money," he said. "And it's not just the sandbags. We can't find workers to lay them. Everyone is either busy or has fled."

Thailand had suffered from torrential rains. But human error compounded the problem as officials allowed the water to build up behind dam walls, only releasing the water once it became clear that the dams would not hold, resulting in a wall of water flowing south. Rapid and poorly planned development had blanketed the floodplain with concrete and tarmac, thus reducing or blocking natural flow patterns. There was also little cooperation between government agencies and municipal officials. Local leaders meanwhile built walls to push the floodwaters into neighboring areas, only for the walls to be sabotaged by those same neighbors.

Fortunately, Every lived in one of the wealthier parts of the city where the government had opted to build embankments, and these diverted the floods toward poorer suburbs with fewer resources for either embankments or pumps. His apartment escaped unscathed, but much of the city did not.

One of those areas was Don Mueang, the country's second airport. I spoke with Somchai, a concierge at the airport's Amari

Airport hotel, who was working there at the time of the floods.[11] "Three weeks. That's how long I was living at this hotel," he says in response to my question. "There were no guests, but someone had to look after the building." Walking outside, he showed me where the floodwaters reached, pointing to a level just above his knee, enough to flood the hotel lobby. And his own house? "Flooded." Like other residents of the city, Somchai was unable to return to his house for many weeks.

What happened in Bangkok as a result of floods could well affect businesses and supply chains in many other cities around the region. A landmark 2011 academic study detailed the world's cities most exposed to flood risk. The killer statistic was the ranking of cities in terms of population exposed to coastal flooding. It is cities in the East that account for seven out of today's top ten, specifically Mumbai, Guangzhou, Shanghai, Ho Chi Minh City, Kolkata, Alexandria, and Tianjin, many of which are major commercial and financial centers.[12] Worse yet, by 2070, the figure would rise to nine out of ten with Bangkok and Yangon being added to the list.

Many Asian cities are built on river deltas and floodplains, which by definition are at low elevations, often close to sea level. Worse, many cities have been built on marshes and clays prone to subsidence under the weight of all the concrete and steel. Just take a look at Bangkok's cracked pavements and building foundations as the city gradually sinks. Worsening floods are also a result of climate change generating greater extremes—more rain in less time and higher storm tides.

Rapid development compounds matters. Officials are reluctant to prevent construction or enforce regulations and standards, often owing to corruption in the property sector. The result is dense urban environments with insufficient permeable surfaces. That's okay if there are sufficient and well-maintained storm drains, but often there are not. In fact, a good test of a city's flood defenses is to count the number of storm drains from a taxi window while driving along any major road in a big city. I'm always surprised at the number of cities that have too few, if any, obvious drains.

The challenge was brought into stark focus in Beijing during the summer of 2012. Here is a city that is China's showcase, the jewel in the crown after a decade of massive construction. Yet, when floods struck in July 2012 as a result of torrential rainfall, the city quickly went underwater, killing some 79 people. The rainfall was the heaviest in over 60 years. However, the city suffered because the drainage system, dating to the 1950s, was built to poor design standards made worse by a lack of maintenance and upgrades. The city's rapid growth had also filled in the canals and waterways that once helped funnel rainwater out of the city.

The economic cost of Thailand's floods was high, estimated by the World Bank at $45 billon.[13] Insurance premiums on industrial factories more than doubled, even as insurers reduced the amount of coverage. Foreign factories were left operating with limited coverage in 2013 even as work on flood prevention projects remained unfinished. Premiums on commercial property in Bangkok also rose steeply, a change from past practice when flood coverage was provided almost free of charge, suggesting that insurers had either faith in climate change or a lack of faith in the government's ability to prevent its implications. Not even Bangkok was safe anymore.

Higher insurance premiums are just one consequence. Banks will also need to think more seriously about the risks of lending to residential apartments built along coastlines or on floodplains, especially if their owners find it tough to insure the full value of their properties. Indeed, this isn't a challenge only for residential properties but also for factories, as many were left uninsured in the immediate aftermath of Bangkok's floods, even among the big multinationals. And banks and insurance providers are both likely to demand more investment in flood prevention before they approve any application.

The cost of building infrastructure will also grow as more is spent on bigger drainage networks and flood defenses, in turn creating demand for engineers and construction companies with experience in these areas. In this, the West has much to offer the East; while the East's cities are most exposed to floods, those in the West certainly have their own challenges, most recently demonstrated by the floods that battered New York City and its surrounding areas in October 2012. And many innovative Western companies would find a market in the East for their products if they were re-engineered at a more affordable price.

IT IS EASY TO FALL IN LOVE WITH THE EAST'S GREAT CITIES. THE REGION stretches across half the globe, from Beijing in the east to Istanbul in the west. In between are some of the world's largest and oldest cities, home to half the world's population and all connected by a single landmass. From Hong Kong, a short five-hour flight puts you in easy reach of Beijing's Forbidden City and relics of imperial China, Myanmar's breathtaking Bagan, or India's spellbinding Hindu temple complexes in Trichy, to name just a few. The East is a fabulously rich mix of cultures, ethnicities, and religions.

Yet it is also tough to ignore the gritty challenges. It seems impossible that the region's urban population will grow by 1.5 billion people without some cities struggling, and I would expect local and international disparities to widen further, such as those between Guangzhou and Changde or between Mumbai and Shanghai.

Wealth is not a sign of immunity, with Hong Kong an ideal example. The city has a GDP per capita of $37,000, and average incomes are nearly three times higher than those in urban mainland China. The city also has fantastic infrastructure and an unemployment rate of 3.5 percent. And yet a survey by Gallup, an American polling company, assessing potential net migration of 135 countries worldwide in 2009, ranked Hong Kong alongside Iraq, Mexico, and Lithuania. For all the city's success, a large number of Hong Kong nationals stated that, faced by rising income inequality, soaring home prices, and worsening air pollution, they would emigrate given the opportunity.

Nor are floods the only natural threat to the region's cities. Air pollution is equally threatening to the building of livable and productive cities as much of the region chokes on smog. Data from the World Health Organization measuring air pollution in 1,100 cities around the world show that cities in the East account for 93 of the top 100 cities most affected by concentrations of PM10, the air pollutant with the most significant health effects and most easily measured across all cities in the region. Of these, cities in China, India, Pakistan, Iran, and Turkey are among the worst offenders, and they are also sadly some of the region's most populous countries.

These challenges, of course, also create opportunities. Filtered water and air purifier equipment are increasingly popular in Hong Kong and are a major outlay for households. Most of the city's taxis are gas powered, but there are also a small but growing number of hybrid versions on the streets. Hong Kong is less affected by floods, but in cities that are vulnerable, there has been increased demand for waterproofing technologies and more complex engineering services intended to secure foundations—among a range of goods and services designed in the West but increasingly appropriate for the East.

History also suggests that most cities will struggle to fund themselves. Even those with enough cash may spend it poorly. If so, that will open doors to private firms stepping in where the state cannot. Take Beaconhouse, the Pakistani private education company providing British-style schooling to 200,000 students. In the autumn of 2011, I visited the company's Educators franchise in Lahore, a low-cost version of the high-end Beaconhouse schools, but providing quality primary-school education for as little as $25 per month. My first thought while standing in front of a classroom of happy eight-year-olds is how other parts of the East might benefit from more private-sector education options.

The idea of focusing only on countries, rather than on regions or city clusters, is also weakened as a result of the East's growing integration. Opening branches in Guangzhou and its neighboring cities, for instance, might be matched by a strategy that focuses on the Greater Mekong, capturing demand in the region's capital cities and, increasingly, midsized cities, with the dual strategies offering a hedge against economic problems in one region or the rise of a robust local competitor in another. Either way, as the region's commercial opportunities mature, so should commercial strategies.

Looking forward, focusing on cities rather than on countries will also be increasingly important as individual cities adopt different strategies for dealing with the challenges of urbanization. This will be especially important as growth rates slow across the region, making it more challenging to fund big infrastructure projects. As demand for more participative democracy rises, local officials will be under pressure to delay or reverse major policy decisions. In fact, the size of many of the region's cities already argues for such a selective strategy given that the scale of some cities, such as Guangzhou, is already big enough to sustain citywide retail chains and restaurant franchises.

The East's urbanization is ultimately a counterpoint to the region's rising middle class. In the end, the cities that consumers live in will also determine what they buy and how they buy. And while local tastes are important, a decent transportation network or public housing system can have an equally big impact on consumer trends.

8

A WATER AND ENERGY NEXUS

THE NEED FOR SUSTAINABLE GROWTH

THE TRAFFIC IN DOHA WAS JAMMED AS STORM DRAINS STRUGGLED to deal with the unexpectedly heavy rain. Friends later reported having to scramble for buckets as their homes sprang leaks. That afternoon I met with a local academic at the Texas A&M University in Qatar who was also a specialist in the country's water desalinization. I arrived late as my car had trouble navigating the traffic and flooded streets. But the academic simply smiled and shrugged it off. "My daughter woke up this morning, saw the rain, and immediately asked me whether she had to go school," he said. Qatari children apparently treat rainfall much as American or British children treat unexpected snowfall.

To be fair, it was the first time it had rained in the Qatari capital that year, and it was already December 12; the city had received no rainfall for at least 345 days.

The small state juts out into the Persian Gulf, connected only by a bridge to Saudi Arabia. Its interior is mainly desert scrub or mudflat, and there are no mountains or natural rivers, meaning the population of 1.9 million survives almost entirely on desalinated water. I was visiting to find out what a country does when it runs out of water. Of course, Qatar is an extreme example. The country receives just over three inches of rain each year; I have sat through tropical thunderstorms in Hong Kong that produce more than that in a day. The rain does recharge the country's groundwater, but much evaporates quickly.

Qatar's economy has grown rapidly in the past 30 years, with its population tripling during that period. Many are migrant workers either helping to construct the city's soaring skyline or signing investment deals in air-conditioned offices. But the implication is the same. There are more mouths than ever to feed but little farmland on which to grow crops to feed them. It is an unpleasant trajectory that means the country must import an ever-increasing quantity of food. It is a reason the government has set up a specialist agriculture fund, Hassad Foods, to do just that and to ensure the country's future.

Qatar is not alone. Most of the East is short of water. It's popular to refer to aircraft carriers, reserve currencies, or a seat on the United Nations Security Council as a measure of a country's global power. Yet the imbalance between a generally water-poor East and a water-rich West deserves as much attention, if not more.

The comparison is stark. America and Europe have a median 12,800 and 7,500 cubic yards of renewable water per person, respectively, as against the East's median 3,700 cubic yards. Of course, some countries perform better than others, but some 18 out of the region's nearly 50 countries have less than 2,600 cubic yards of renewable water per person. Moreover, certain cities and regions in the West do face water shortages. Nevertheless, the West would profit handsomely if it could export water much as it exports grain. (In fact, there are plenty of Western companies that do export water, such as Evian and Pellegrino, but they aren't about to make up for the shortages.)

Those shortages mean that the East's economic rise already faces greater challenges than did the West during its own economic development, and that's before considering the impact of climate change on today's global economy. No discussion of the region's future can discount the possibility that some cities, or even countries, will run up against serious water shortages over the coming decade. That has implications for companies in the region, especially manufacturers. But it also has implications for governments trying to manage the expectations of a rising middle class.

Metito understands these challenges. The Dubai-based firm lies just a 45-minute flight from Doha and has operations in Bahrain, Egypt, China, and Indonesia, to name just a few countries. Farouk Ghandour, the firm's Lebanese founder, established the firm in Beirut over 50 years ago, and Metito has grown steadily since.

I first met Rami Ghandour, the company's Managing Director, in Hong Kong in the summer of 2012. Ghandour is a regular visitor to the city and also to many of mainland China's less well-known cities where Metito has operations. The firm's wastewater treatment plant in Nanchang, the capital of southern Jiangxi province, is situated not far from China's largest, and increasingly polluted, freshwater lake. But other plants are spread across the country, including those in the northern cities of Changchun and Panjin, and the central cities of Chuzhou and Changde, none of which are found in a typical English-language travel guide.

However, it wasn't until the following year that I had a chance to visit Metito's headquarters in Dubai. The building itself is worth a tour as a trailblazer for the region's resource efficiency. Built using recycled materials and designed to reuse water and conserve energy, the building was the first in the Middle East to be gold certified by the US Green Building Council. In fact, Metito's headquarters arguably have more in common with Dubai's traditional houses—designed to withstand a harsh climate—than they do with the emirate's glass-clad skyscrapers that house much of the business community.

Ghandour had just arrived on the overnight red-eye flight from Beirut. "It was the first time my plane flew around Syria, rather than across the southern provinces. That's not a good sign," he remarked.[1] Water shortages aren't the cause of Syria's unrest, but they might prolong it if nothing is done to reduce consumption.

I valued the company's view as Metito is one of the few to be involved in water treatment across the East and deals with water-poor countries on a daily basis. Consider some of the company's more important markets: China has just 2,700 cubic yards of renewable water per person, or one-third the median figure for the West; India has even less at 2,000 cubic yards; Egypt is among the most water deprived at just 900 cubic yards. In each of these countries, water treatment and recycling isn't just about protecting ecosystems, as it sometimes appears to be in the West; it is a decision of survival.[2]

So I had one big question for Ghandour: why isn't the region doing more to solve its water shortages, given that it's no secret the East is water-poor and that the technologies already exist to treat and recycle water? Surely governments must look into the future and be worried about what they see.

Ghandour sees several issues. The first is tariffs. "Water is too cheap in most parts of the East. There's no economic motivation to conserve," he says. "Take where I live in Dubai. If you drive around the neighborhood at night you can typically tell which families are expatriates and which are locals just by looking at their house—the locals have dozens of lights on and very green gardens to water," says Ghandour, referring to the fact that utilities are largely free for Emiratis.

Then there's conservation education. "We are inefficient users of water across the region. In the Gulf, we have higher per capita water consumption than in America, in spite of the fact the region is water-poor. So there is huge scope to reduce demand through better water education. For example, have people been brought up with the simple concept of, 'Do you turn the taps off when brushing your teeth, or do you keep the water running the whole time?'" he tells me.

The lack of a single template is also challenging. "Each country has its own challenges," says Ghandour. "There are truly excellent technical specialists in India, and our own global engineering center is in Pune. The people are also very hardworking, just as hard as the Chinese. But it takes a long time to get anything done in the country, mainly because of bureaucracy. China also has good engineers, but decisions are made faster. There's also a greater tendency to work for the collective good and to meet deadlines. In the Gulf, it's another issue entirely, as transient populations weaken civic responsibility," Ghandour says.

Metito is one of the few firms to have built thriving businesses along the full breadth of the Silk Road region. Its experience is instructive, as the firm has expanded gradually over the past five decades, but today has more than 2,500 employees, including 600 in Egypt, 200 in China, 200 in Indonesia, and another 100 in India, among other countries. Senior managers are typically local and have worked for the firm for years, rotating through the head office periodically. "We don't want to roll out a global template. It makes it more difficult at the beginning, but more sustainable in the long term," says Ghandour.

That is especially critical to the water-treatment industry, as the firm has to adapt to the local challenges of treating water, such as freshwater from Egypt's Nile River or the discharge from a chemical plant near the inland Chinese city of Chongqing. Two of Metito's operations offer an example of the type of challenges faced by the company, and the region itself, in improving its water networks.

In Jakarta, the Indonesian capital, Metito won a contract in 2006 to manage the water supply for the city's main port, Tanjung Priok, as well as three other ports. Water is critical to a port's productivity, as ships need to refill their water tanks while docked. But Tanjung Priok was struggling to guarantee a reliable supply, and ships were docking at Singapore's ports just to refill with water before sailing onward to Jakarta. "Some 56 percent of the port's water was lost through the network either as a result of leakage or theft. This is a great example of poor management," says Ghandour.

Yet the solution was simple. By repairing the leaks and putting systems in place to prevent theft, Metito cut that figure to just 11 percent by December 2006, only six months after they took over the port's water contract. "And we did it without heavy investment. We just focused on fixing the simple things," says Ghandour.

And this is in a city that already suffers from water shortages. Jakarta's groundwater has fallen by nearly 100 feet in the past 50 years as a result of so many private wells being dug. The decline has contributed to floods in coastal areas of the city, even as some households have seen their well-water supply dry up as newly constructed residential developments suck up the local groundwater. For the worst affected, water is rationed, forcing some households to search for water. The frustration then is that the solutions, at least at Jakarta's port, can be as simple as plugging holes and preventing theft.

It's a point Ghandour is keen to emphasize. "The technologies are already available to conserve water. In fact, often they are relatively simple solutions. It's the application that is challenging, such as our experience in Jakarta. The problem is working in a local context and getting results."

Closer to home, the firm faced a different situation at its sewage treatment plant at the nearby Dubai Investment Park. I visited the plant shortly after speaking with Ghandour and was met by Samer Yousef, Metito's Senior O&M Manager.[3] Yousef spoke passionately about the plant's operations before offering a tour of the site itself. The plant was built in stages over ten years and used everything from cost-effective aerobic treatment, a popular 100-year-old technology, to high-tech filtration membranes. "We are a showcase for a range of technologies," he said as we tried to keep out of the sun during one of Dubai's scorching summer days.

But it's where the sewage ends up that matters. Much of the treated water is used to water the gardens that make Dubai Investment Park look surprisingly green even during the height of Dubai's 95-degree summers. "It looks like California," Ghandour warns me before I set off for the site. And he's right.

Using treated sewage water to keep Dubai green makes a great deal of sense in this water-poor country. Why pour drinking water onto the city's gardens? While the water from the Metito plant is fully recycled, not all of Dubai's treated wastewater is being reused, and a share is dumped into the sea by the local municipality, underscoring that although the technologies to treat water are available, the bigger challenge is often finding the right incentives. Still, the emirate's leadership has recognized the problem and is forcing change: for instance, the water regulator only recently introduced legislation requiring all district cooling plants to use recycled water.

Maybe attitudes toward water will only change once the water runs out. Then, the idea of either conserving water, such as at Jakarta's ports, or using recycled water, such as at Dubai Investment Park, will make more sense. But for now, much of the region appears to be running on the belief that water will always be available.

LIVING IN HONG KONG MAKES ONE APPRECIATE RELIABLE WATER AND ENERGY. First, the average resident takes a 14-minute shower each day and often multiple showers, especially during the summer.[4] Second, power outages are rare, but they matter when living in one of the city's 40-story buildings, as a walk up those stairs in the middle of summer can demonstrate. So trying to imagine a Hong Kong where water and power shortages are commonplace makes the city seem unlivable. The same is true for many of the region's fast-growing cities, whether it's Dubai, Singapore, or Shanghai.

The linkage between water and power is often overlooked, and yet it is critical: the typical city consumes more water in order to generate power than it does to wash dishes or flush toilets.[5] So if a city starts to suffer from water shortages, there is a chance it may also suffer from power outages.

Energy production is a massive consumer of water mainly because it is used for cooling and other process-related purposes. The typical thermal power plant—such as a coal-based or nuclear power plant— withdraws water from a nearby lake or river in order to condense the steam used to generate electricity. The amount of water withdrawn and consumed might depend on the technologies used, but thermal power plants are the biggest industrial users of water in an increasingly water-scarce world. And so a country that is water-poor is also likely to be energy-hungry, suffering from shortages of both.

This matters in the East. The region has less than half the median water resources of the West, yet its growth rates are twice as fast. So how will the East power its homes and factories even as a rapidly urbanizing population consumes more of the region's limited water supplies? Consider what might happen if power shortages were to force factories to lay off workers even as water shortages left households with less water to drink, flush toilets, or wash clothes. For populations with rising expectations of their government, elected or unelected, the results could be messy (and dirty).

New technologies will certainly help to reduce the energy sector's water consumption, such as fitting power plants with dry cooling systems and retiring some of the world's more inefficient plants. But the sector is losing a race against rising demand, and the International Energy Agency (IEA) forecasts that the energy sector's global water withdrawals will rise 20 percent by 2035. Moreover, alternative fuels are not a simple solution as most biofuels require water for irrigating feedstocks, and fuel conservation and investment in wind and solar power are not taking place fast enough.

There is another alternative: using less energy, not more. Dr. Fatih Birol, Chief Economist for the IEA, intimated as much to reporters in 2012 when he argued that the world would require a range of energy sources in the coming years, saying, "But if I were placing bets, my bet would be on energy efficiency."

The numbers underscore the reason: by investing in energy efficiency, the agency estimates that the growth rate of the world's energy demand would halve by 2035. What does the agency mean by energy efficiency? They are referring to measures that reduce consumption while providing the same level of service. For instance, buying a more efficient air conditioner that uses less electricity to keep the room at the same temperature, as opposed to simply raising the temperature on the old model and sweating it out in order to conserve power. (Both are good strategies for cutting energy demand, though the former is the more comfortable option.)

Better yet, energy efficiency eventually pays for itself. The IEA estimates that $11.8 trillion of investment in energy efficiency is needed by

2035 in order to cut energy demand growth in half, but this saves the consumer $17.5 trillion in energy costs during the same period.

It's a no-brainer, right? Energy efficiency both reduces water consumption and eventually saves costs. That's critical for a rising East given the region's rapid industrialization combined with its worsening water scarcities. And yet, convincing firms to actually green-light energy efficiency projects is a major challenge. "It's the no-brainer that never happens," says Glen Plumbridge, echoing many in the industry.[6] Much like Metito's Ghandour, he argues that there are already plenty of tried and tested technologies for conserving energy. The challenge is getting companies to care enough to do something about the problem.

Plumbridge is Hong Kong Managing Director for Sustainable Development Capital LLP (SDCL), a specialist financial company with an investment team that focuses exclusively on the energy efficiency sector with offices in London, New York, and Hong Kong.

I ask why companies are reluctant. "Understandably, most firms focus their resources and energy on their core business and growth of the business. Firms also don't always have the knowledge and expertise to identify the energy efficiency opportunities. And even if they identify opportunities, then many run into additional internal barriers such as allocation of budget to these projects," he says. "All that means most don't treat energy efficiency as a priority and so don't allocate internal resources, whether staff or capital, to implement the projects."

In 2012, researchers at Imperial College London surveyed CFOs from 30 multinational firms on the subject. Over half of the respondents saw such investments as less risky than their core business investments. And yet, over 80 percent of respondents demanded the same or an even higher rate of return on their energy efficiency investments. Why? Due to the multiyear payback periods involved or to their unwillingness to carry the projects on their balance sheet. Compounding the problem, few firms have the internal capacity to evaluate, recognize, or accept cash flows from energy efficiency projects.

I can sympathize with the challenges. We changed our family's lightbulbs a few years ago, buying LED lights from one of the many lighting shops in Hong Kong's busy Wan Chai district. At $36 a bulb, I found myself quizzing the store owners on refunds and warranties. For its $3 alternative, I wouldn't have bothered. When the savings can be counted in cents each month, it's tough to consider the long-term financial benefit. For a factory, the gains are larger. But for an operations manager more focused on keeping his plants running, considering a $1 million investment is a time-consuming exercise.

And that's where the Singaporean government steps in by introducing the right incentives for change. The government's Economic Development Board (EDB) recently selected SDCL to establish a pilot program to fund energy efficient investments in the manufacturing sector. Under the program, SDCL will fund energy efficient investments worth up to $200 million, paid purely by the energy cost savings. The Singaporean government has also recently implemented an energy efficiency and conservation act to unify sector-specific standards and target the country's largest energy users.

"Singapore is one of the region's best chances for getting energy efficiency investment rolling out on a large scale," says Plumbridge, back in Hong Kong again after one of his weekly visits to the city-state. "The Singaporean government has a clear policy underpinned by legislation, that in turn is supported by multiple coordinated strategies and grants to support the country's drive for greater efficiency. Singapore also has the benefit of a good legal system and transparency essential for the implementation of a private investment program in energy efficiency," he adds. In effect, the Singaporean government is making people prioritize energy efficiency.

SINGAPORE IS AN ADMIRABLE LEADER, AS IS OFTEN THE CASE, BUT CHINA has dozens of Singapore-sized economies, and many more small- to midsized cities. How applicable is the Singapore model to those cities? Can Beijing's state planners force change, or will Chinese municipal leaders take up the challenge?

There is certainly motivation. China's water resources are on a par with those in the rest of the region. The problem is that the country's resources are unevenly distributed: the southern regions receive significantly more water than the northern regions, whether because of more regular rainfall or runoff from the Himalayan plateau. In fact, the northern regions have about the same water resources as Egypt on a per capita basis. That's a scary thought: it means that over 250 million Chinese people, or about the same number of people as live in the Middle East, are existing on water resources similar to those of Egypt.

Worse yet, coal-fired power accounts for 77 percent of the country's power generation, as compared to 37 percent in the United States.[7] Much of that coal is also extracted in the northern regions where water is scarce, further straining the country's water resources. Nuclear power, by contrast, accounts for just one percent of the country's power generation and is a similarly thirsty consumer of water. Moreover, the rapid growth of the inland regions means more power plants relying on lakes and rivers, rather than seawater, for cooling purposes. In short, it's one big headache for a rapidly growing country.

"People are living a fairy tale," says Terry Foecke.[8] "Most believe they have access to water and just can't conceive of what's coming. The assumption is that the government will step up and deal with water shortages if they happen. But by then, it may be too late." It's a none-too-subtle warning on the risks of ignoring water scarcity.

But then Foecke knows what he is talking about. Based in Shenzhen, Foecke is Head of Supplier Development for PCH International and spends much of his time making factory visits across China, helping factory owners improve their production process. "Eighty percent of factories are stuck," he says. "They want to change, but don't know how. There are no industrial consulting reports to refer to, and the factories often don't trust the local consultants. So that's where we step in to help them understand how simple changes to the production process or new equipment can make big cost savings."

He tells a story that sums up many of China's challenges. "A few years back I met with a factory in Foshan, near Guangzhou, producing for export. They were doing OK and had invested in energy-efficient equipment, so they weren't the bad guys. But then the local government pulled their license and told them to leave. Some developer wanted to build a residential complex nearby and install clothes dryers in each unit in order to hike the sales price. But there just wasn't enough power to supply both the factory and the complex. So the local government made a choice and told the factory to go."

Foecke has plenty of other stories to tell about China's looming energy crunch. "Drive around the region and you can see factories that make you ask, what's that doing here? There's no obvious water. But the factory has drilled a well. And the well goes deeper as the water table drops by more than 100 meters [300 feet]. Sure, factories could treat wastewater, but it's cheaper for a factory to drill a well. There aren't the incentives yet to force factories to treat water. There's not economic motivation," he says. So what's next, I ask? "I can see a train wreck coming, and perhaps that is when the factories finally act," he replies.

And yet there are bright spots. "There are deeply nationalistic factory owners who are doing everything they can to conserve energy," Foecke says. "These will be the firms that will be best positioned in the global market when the crunch comes."

Foecke describes one such factory where a banner above the factory floor reads: *Every RMB matters. Wasted material means wasted lives.* Based in Guangdong province, the factory produces many of the metal parts used by IKEA in its cabinet and wardrobe frames. "It's a family-owned company originally from Hubei and the owners pay attention to every detail, from the regional food they serve in the canteen to their tight control over the manufacturing process," says Foecke. "They figured out that water and energy shortages are likely to arrive faster than people think, and so they try and squeeze gains wherever they can."

Often the solutions are simple, such as enclosing the paint room on the factory floor with a separate roof and walls. While that is common practice for an automobile manufacturer, it is less common for a midsized manufacturer where painting typically takes place in an unsealed area of the factory floor. But the change enabled the factory to regulate the air quality in the paint room rather than having to use large energy-intensive fans to move air around the entire factory floor. It also had the additional benefit of improving product quality, as paints were applied at a consistent temperature.

The IEA would be pleased to see the results. Their estimates suggest that these sorts of measures could help China make energy savings worth 25 percent equivalent to 2010 energy, far greater than the possible 15 percent savings predicted in the United States and 13 percent in Europe.

Of course, China's leadership recognizes the problem and is responding. For instance, the country's latest five-year plan targets ambitious gains in water and energy efficiency. Moreover, much of China's vast debt spending over the past five years was used for water-related projects. I was struck by this during 2011 when we dug through hundreds of bond prospectuses issued by local government-linked special-purpose vehicles. Time and again, the details were related to water conservation and water treatment. Bad debts? Most likely. But that spending might also prove critical in the years ahead.

So WHAT WILL IT TAKE FOR CHINA TO CHANGE ITS WATER PRACTICES DRA-matically? China matters because of its size. The idea of the world's second-largest economy running into water shortages is a scary one. Indeed, among the world's top five major economic powers—America, China, Japan, Germany, and France—only China is seriously water-poor, and if even the idea of China's economy slowing below 8 percent in 2013 was enough to seriously spook financial markets, then the idea of worsening water shortages would have an even greater impact as rising unemployment and inflation took its toll on households.

Hong Kong then offers its larger neighbor a benchmark for the risks. Take a look at any bathroom in Hong Kong, and there are two sets of pipes: the ceramic pipes are for clean water and the plastic pipes are for saltwater used for flushing toilets.

In the 1950s, Hong Kong first toyed with the idea of dual plumbing. By the 1960s, the city had no choice as droughts resulted in widespread water rationing. Households had access to water for just four hours every four days, a situation difficult to imagine in today's modern city. But 50 years ago, Hong Kong was reliant on its own small reservoirs and natural rainfall, unable to import large volumes of water from the mainland owing to political tensions between Communist China and British-ruled Hong Kong. And so the Hong Kong government acted as the result of lack of choice, making dual-pipe plumbing mandatory in new buildings.

The experience offers two lessons for China. The first is that Hong Kong didn't retrofit its buildings with dual plumbing, a far more expensive option. Instead, most of the city's residential apartments and hotels were built after the change in regulations, so dual plumbing was installed as buildings were constructed.

China is a unique situation as the country has yet to construct a sizeable share of its building stock. That makes it much cheaper to build residential apartments with dual plumbing rather than retrofit at a later date. The same is true for the country's manufacturing sector, where factories are constantly buying new equipment as they look to improve the efficiency of their manufacturing process. Ensuring that developers and manufacturers are investing in water- and energy-efficient equipment is more effective than waiting until the crunch hits. Hong Kongers might take multiple showers a day, but a 50-year-old decision to use saltwater to flush toilets aids the city's water efficiency.

The second lesson, however, is that Hong Kong's water shortages coincided with a period of social unrest as migrants flooded into the city and growing prosperity bred corruption in turn. And this was before the rise of a genuine middle class, a growing sense of democratic rights, and the spread of online media.

What might happen in China were entire cities restricted to just four hours of water every four days? There is no serious modern precedent. But even the threat of water contamination has brought people into the streets. In July 2002, for instance, mass protests erupted in Nantong, an eastern coastal city in Jiangsu province, over fears that construction of a paper manufacturing facility would contaminate the city's drinking-water source. Nantong's Communist Party Chief was stripped naked, according to reports, and a police car was turned upside down. The municipal government canceled the project the same day.

MAYBE CHINA IS FACING A TRAIN WRECK, AND THE WATER WILL RUN OUT. But just as China's future water shortages might damage the world economy, so might the country's progress toward greater water and energy efficiency help the rest of the world, especially the developing world, tackle its own shortages. That is not to say that China will provide a simple template for the rest of the world to follow. In fact, the country might yet face severe water and energy shortages in spite of its best efforts. But the commercial spillover of those efforts to the rest of the world is already significant.

The government's ability to intervene through the state sector is one important benefit. It is Chinese state firms that have made the heaviest investments in water and energy conservation, partly in response to government dictates and privileged access to capital. In turn, this helps innovative private-sector firms to build scale.

Take LanzaTech, a clean-tech firm that has developed bacteria to convert waste gas, or carbon monoxide, into biofuels and chemicals. LanzaTech's technologies were first developed in New Zealand, before a consortium of US and, later, Chinese venture capitalists bought into the firm and took it to China, where it now partners with two major Chinese steel manufacturers, Baosteel and Capital Steel. "There are not too many places you can scale technology like this. Outside of China, India is perhaps the only other place," says Dr. James Zhang, a consultant to the firm and founder of Formation 8, a venture capital company.[9]

It is understandable that small private firms might look to China for dollars and scale. However, the leading multinationals are also using China as a strategic bridgehead to the rest of the world. Among those, it is the Honeywell story that is especially compelling. In 2012, Honeywell appointed its China CEO as head of the High Growth Regions, a group that includes Brazil, Russia, India, and China, as well as Indonesia, Malaysia, Thailand, and Vietnam. For all the talk about the rise of the BRICs, it is often little more than talk. So asking Honeywell's China

CEO to lead the firm's push into the world's other fast-growing markets felt refreshingly real world.

The logic goes like this: Honeywell's products, when re-engineered for China at a lower price point, are likely to sell well in the world's other fast-growing markets. Some of those products include energy management systems to measure plant performance or combustion control; high-efficiency combustion systems; Smart Grid solutions to manage their power consumption; biofuel technologies to help convert organic waste into fuel; and LED lighting. It only made sense for Honeywell China to lead the charge, given that it was the firm's Chinese engineers who were doing most of the re-engineering.

I visited some of those 1,400 China-based engineers in the summer of 2013, touring the firm's campus-style facilities in Shanghai's Pudong district. "We're completely out of space," said Jason Lo, the Head of Strategy for China, signing me through security.[10] The facilities were a mix of offices and cubicle workstations. Mainly young engineers worked behind their computers in an open-plan office that ringed a central core of laboratories, each assigned to a specific department and allowing the engineers to test their prototypes before sending design changes to the firm's fabricators in the southern city of Shenzhen.

Outsourcing to China to produce cheap exports isn't a new idea. But Honeywell was instead benchmarking itself against Chinese competitors for sale to the China market. "We can now design products at prices matching the leading Chinese firms," says Lo. "The next challenge is getting to a price point for the mass market."

The process is harder than it looks, but there are clear rewards. Lo had only just returned from Istanbul, Turkey's capital and the historical bridge between Asia and Europe. He had spent a week in the city working alongside Honeywell colleagues to identify which products re-engineered by the firm's Shanghai-based engineers might be suitable for the Turkish market. "We ended up picking a series of products that are about 30 percent cheaper than their European equivalents. We are maintaining our existing products to target the high end of the market in Turkey, and using lower-cost Chinese alternatives to tap the middle to low end where price sensitivity is greater."

I was struck that he had chosen Turkey, rather than a closer Asian neighbor. "The local regulations are more straightforward, at least as an initial step," Lo answered. "Turkey also has a lot of contractors that go outside the country, so the country would be a nice hub for us to export goods." This is a fair point, given that Turkish construction companies are already competing fiercely with the Chinese in Africa and Central Asia, and they would probably welcome the chance to level the playing field, even if they couldn't offer the same low labor costs or cheap debt financing.

Honeywell's experience isn't a solution for the region's water and energy shortages. Ultimately, it is local economics, such as energy costs and tariff rates, as well as consumer awareness, that is critical to a country's ability to conserve and recycle water. However, Honeywell's engineers are benefiting from China's growing interest in water and energy efficiency and then using the country's spending on such projects and economies of scale to their advantage. In doing so, they are finding ways to make energy efficiency cheaper for the rest of the world. It's a small but useful step.

Honeywell's starting point might be different, but it shares much with Metito in its final trajectory. One is a local firm that took itself global. The other is a global firm that went local. But, critically, they both understand the importance of adapting a global platform to local conditions. Metito brings Indian engineers from its research facilities in Pune to China to introduce best practices from one developing country to another. Honeywell in turn sends Chinese managers to Turkey to find ways to export products engineered for the Chinese market to other parts of the developing world.

OF THE CHALLENGES DESCRIBED IN THIS BOOK, THE NEXUS OF WATER AND energy seems the most intractable. Sure, there are success stories at the level of individual companies, but the region isn't responding fast enough to the looming challenges. What's needed for the change?

Metito's Ghandour rightly argues the importance of economics; energy costs and tariff rates, for instance, must reach a punitive level that forces factories and households to conserve. However, while governments often have little difficulty charging market rates to commercial users, such as factories or offices, they find it far harder charging the same rates to households. Rising utility bills can hurt spending and damage support for either single-party states, such as China, or multi-party states like India, so long as there are a large number of households that are only just making ends meet.

"People don't have enough data," argues Foecke, offering another key influence. "You need data in order to prove efficiency gains and cost savings, otherwise people will just talk and talk, and decisions are made on the basis of who can talk loudest, rather than the gains that can be made. For now, there just isn't enough data available in China." I think back to my experience buying LED lights in Hong Kong. If only the shopkeeper had had a pamphlet showing me the relative cost savings of LED versus ordinary lights. He didn't, and I bought purely on faith that the technology actually works.

Energy and water shortages will change the region's growth outlook. Shortages will create a long-term drain on economic activity, especially in countries suffering from periodic drought. That might appear overly bearish, but it's difficult to see the region's investment in efficiency rising faster than its consumption of water and energy. That said, shortages will also add back to growth where firms are investing in new equipment, thus creating commercial opportunities. China is especially likely to soften any slowing of investment in traditional sectors through greater spending on more efficient equipment.

LanzaTech is just one firm that has benefited from China's challenges. But there are many others, such as Wasabi Energy, an Australian company selling an energy-conversion technology that converts the type of industrial heat produced by cement or steel factories into energy. By 2013, the company had won a series of contracts across China, including one from Sinopec, a major oil company. The ability to tap China's scale, as well as the deep pockets of state-owned companies, had helped the company to build scale even as it sold its products to other parts of the East, including Pakistan, Turkey, and the UAE.

There are also opportunities even in sectors where Chinese firms are popularly seen as already competitive. Take the solar industry as an example. China accounts for a large share of the world's production of solar cells and PV modules and is a major exporter in these products. And yet, America is itself a large exporter of the capital equipment used in the solar manufacturing process. For instance, GT Advanced Technologies, a major American equipment and services provider to both the solar and LED sector, earns 95 percent of its revenues in Asia, of which China accounts for over half the total.[11]

For foreign companies operating outside the clean-tech industry there is also reason to pay attention to the growing risks of water and energy shortages to protect against business disruption. Leading firms are already examining their exposure on a country-by-country and even city-by-city basis, investing in recycled sources as a hedge against future shortages or sudden changes in government policy, especially in China. Ultimately, pressure to conserve is a matter of survival for the East, and the region is more likely to experience rapid change rather than the more gradual path that the West has taken over the past few decades.

9

CONCLUSION

IN THE WINTER OF 2012, EGYPTIAN STRAWBERRIES SUDDENLY APPEARED for sale in supermarkets across Hong Kong, replacing the usual American varieties. Egypt isn't the first place I think of when looking to buy strawberries, so I was naturally struck by their appearance. By chance, I had previously met with a veteran farm manager working for Driscoll's, an American producer of fresh berries and the largest supplier of strawberries globally, while visiting a private farm in southern Guangdong province. I asked about the change as we stood on the roof of the management building to get a better view of the farm's hothouses.

"Sure, Egypt is a big exporter. We even have some farms there," he said in reply. I then asked about the impact from the revolution. "It hasn't affected our farms or shipments."

In fact, Egypt was a more reliable supplier of strawberries than America during that winter. It sounds odd, but then selecting strawberries for export is a laborious process as the berries must be graded according to their ripeness before they are packed for the long journey overseas. Usually that's not a problem, but American berry growers faced a shortage of migrant labor in 2011 partly due to new anti-immigration laws that scared off many workers. For Egyptian producers it was a boon. And even as protestors filled Cairo's Tahrir Square, Egyptian strawberries were squeezing out American varieties in Hong Kong.

The East is one of the world's largest consumers of strawberries and is ripe for further growth. But Egypt's ability to capture market share in Hong Kong during a period of unrest at home neatly illustrates how commercial success can be difficult to predict in an increasingly complex global economy. Trying to pick winners and losers on the basis of GDP, population, or other national measures of growth can help determine national success, but it can also be an unreliable measure of a specific company's performance, especially as the nature of the region's opportunities and risks evolves.

For much of the past few decades, it was possible for a CEO or business owner to have a good "mental map" of the East. Business activity was usually limited to a handful of the region's most developed countries and cities. Few companies had strategies for penetrating the less mature countries, such as Indonesia, or midsized cities, such as China's Hefei. Most of a company's employees were based in Hong Kong or Singapore, not far from the CEO's office. It was a simpler time when a single manager could keep track of operations and make relative judgments with ease.

That's no longer the case. The one complaint I have heard repeatedly from CEOs and business owners over the past few years, irrespective of the company or country, is that the business has grown too big and too unwieldy for a single individual to control. The days of a good mental map are over, and managers are increasingly relying on local input to judge risks and opportunities. But that creates a new set of challenges. Local managers are skilled at evaluating opportunities in their home markets, but who makes the call on whether to open new stores in China's Guangxi province or on Indonesia's Sumatra?

That's a difficult question in the East because, while growth brings opportunities, it almost invariably brings greater complexity. Consider the challenges for foreign retailers selling to consumers in Wuhan and Surabaya, rather than only in Beijing or Jakarta, or for foreign brand owners now sourcing from factories in Bangladesh and Vietnam, rather than just in China.

Each chapter in this book looks at a stand-alone subject, but the complexities also extend between those subjects. Zhao Yingguang's story is one example of how changes in China's manufacturing and retail sectors are converging. Zhao is a 39-year-old serial entrepreneur from the eastern province of Shandong. He returned to China in 2008 after living in Korea for ten years and decided to tap into the growing popularity of Korean design by sourcing Korean fashion clothing for sale in China's online marketplaces, such as Taobao. However, it was a tough business as a result of long lead times and unreliable suppliers.

So Zhao decided to establish his own brand by adapting the latest Korean fashions for local tastes. He then placed small orders with local manufacturers who were able to deliver rapidly. Zhao's HSTYLE is today among the most popular apparel brands on Taobao and is just one of the company's seven brands: it has since branched into menswear and children's clothing. The company today has more than 1,900 employees and 150 suppliers, and while HSTYLE continues to sell its products through online marketplaces such as Taobao, the company has also opened its own official online store.

Zhao has made good use of a number of convergences. First, the expansion of China's e-commerce sales and infrastructure has enabled Zhao to build a business without investing in traditional retail stores, which would be an expensive proposition. Second, rising purchasing power has made China an attractive proposition for local manufacturers wanting to produce for local demand, rather than for export. Near-sourcing has also allowed HSTYLE to develop into a fast-fashion brand, much like H&M, a Swedish multinational retailer, so the company is unlikely to buy from cheaper Bangladesh or Vietnam.

For now, HSTYLE is selling to China, but the idea of young Chinese designers making use of the country's large apparel manufacturing sector to produce small runs of distinct designs for sale on e-commerce platforms across the region is a compelling proposition. Of course, fashions differ between countries. But then why not also employ Indonesian or Malaysian designers who understand local tastes and can adapt the same local Korean designs and perhaps even use factories in those same countries?

The region's improving logistics chains will have to respond in turn. Just as Thailand's upcountry shoppers are changing the way retailers and logistics companies distribute across the country, the rise of e-commerce companies such as HSTYLE will also force change in the way goods are shipped across the East. Express air freight between countries is a natural beneficiary, and local express-freight companies, especially the Chinese players such as SF Express, are likely to emerge as new regional multinationals because they are able to make the linkages between China's big economy and the region.

Local partnerships are increasingly important to tapping local markets

The fact that HSTYLE is competing directly with Korea's fashion industry, rather than with those of France or Italy, is a strong indication of just how robust local competitors have become. And it is this growing interaction between local and foreign companies that is one of the East's biggest sources of complexity. Samsung versus Apple, Chow Tai Fook versus Tiffany, SF Express versus DHL, Walmart versus Vanguard, are all examples of local companies competing effectively not only in their home markets, but also gradually further abroad as they look to build regional or global businesses.

Indeed, when Hollywood's all-powerful studios decide to go local, it is a sign that not even the strongest international brands are strong enough to resist the forces at work. The industry's blockbusters account for just a small share of India's film market, so the American studios are linking up with Indian partners to produce Hindi films, as well as films in local dialects and so tap into the Tamil, Bengali, and other regional markets. Of course, none of this would be possible without strong local partners who enjoy significant autonomy to choose scripts and actors, not an easy step for such big and successful brands.

Hollywood's experience is much the same as that of consumer product firms as they look to tap into local demand. Whereas consumers in Beijing, Shanghai, or Guangzhou are relatively globalized, those in Changsha, Wuhan, and Zhengzhou are not, and it is challenging for foreign companies to target local tastes.

Take recent events in China's retail sector. In 2013, Tesco announced that it would take a 20 percent stake in a joint venture with Vanguard, the country's second-largest retailer and part of China Resources Enterprise. Tesco entered the market in 2004, but the firm's 136 stores had recently been struggling. Vanguard, by contrast, operated over 940 hypermarkets and supermarkets across 58 cities, so the new venture would allow the British retailer to tap into its partner's local relationships and deep understanding of consumer preferences in China's less globalized midsized cities.

For Tesco, the decision made strategic sense given the challenges other foreign retailers faced. Walmart, the big American retailer, was finding it tough when faced with competition not only from Vanguard, but also from Sun Art Retail Group, the country's largest hypermarket operator with 273 stores. Home Depot, an American multinational retailer, announced in September 2012 that it would close all seven of its home-improvement stores in China, while Metro Group, a German diversified multinational retailer, said in January 2013 that it was pulling out of the local consumer electronics business.

However, joint ventures aren't the only solution, especially for midsized firms. In the autumn of 2011, I was involved with a European professional sound equipment company looking to tap into China's growing performance and events industries.[1] Setting up a wholly owned business to sell to the country's large private-sector events industry in Beijing, Shanghai, and Guangzhou made sense. But a local partner was equally invaluable for pitching the company's products to local governments that were building a rash of concert halls in the country's midsized and inland cities where local relationships were critical.

Local competitors are growing in strength, and local consumers are spoilt for choice

Tie-ups with foreign companies can add value to a local business. But a growing number are instead simply acquiring foreign companies and bringing their technologies and management expertise back to the East, thus providing stiff competition to foreign competitors by offering a similar range of products and quality.

Wanda's purchase of AMC Cinemas is the most recent example. The Chinese conglomerate's purchase has effectively shut the door to foreign competition in what will eventually be the world's largest cinema market, as Wanda utilizes its scale and AMC's products to deliver a world-class cinema experience. Or consider the purchase of Aquascutum, a British luxury brand, by YGM Trading, a Hong Kong–based trading company, creating a firm that combines the power of a foreign brand with the market insights of a local firm, potentially making Aquascutum a tough competitor in the region.

The willingness of local companies to acquire or tie up with foreign partners argues for urgency when looking at opportunities in the East. It might have once made sense to delay market entry, but the product range on offer to shoppers in the region is growing daily, so those who wait might find it tough to break into the market.

Consider Hong Kong. Only a decade ago there were still good opportunities acting as a local agent for a foreign brand. Today, it is more common to hear of failures than successes. The market for wines, for instance, is saturated with specialist stores offering a dazzling array of small labels. New labels wanting to enter the market might spend years lobbying hotels and restaurants to be included on wine lists or convincing stores to buy more than a few bottles. It is much the same for the hair products and cosmetics market, where what isn't already available in Hong Kong can be purchased online.

That doesn't mean an end to opportunities. For a start, the region's young Muslim consumers are growing in number and are also unbranded and underserved. There are also niche opportunities, such as marketing organic products, targeting the region's growing food health worries, especially in China.

However, the days of simply offering a better product than a local competitor does are fading fast, especially in the consumer products market. And many foreign companies are increasingly planning their market entry or growth strategies in the East much as they might if they were trying to penetrate markets in America or Europe. That doesn't argue against market entry. It simply calls for a more deliberate strategy of choosing the right country, the right city, and the right income level, as well as asking whether the business structure and product offering are suitable for tapping into local markets.

The willingness of local companies to acquire foreign brands also argues for urgency as the same companies look to build their business in the West. For now, the stronger growth is at home, and companies such as Wanda and YGM Trading are more focused on China than on markets abroad. But should local companies start to exploit their scale and cost base in order to grow their newly acquired brands globally, then multinationals and midsized foreign companies alike might find that a presence in the East is as much a good defensive strategy for home markets as it is an offensive strategy.

Local companies will need support as they develop regional or global brands

Local firms also don't have it all their way. Multinationals are still well placed to build regional businesses, leveraging their brand recognition, as well as larger marketing and distribution networks. So far, there is only a small but growing number of companies in the East repeating the same feat: Shangri-La, the Hong Kong hotel group, and Hyundai, the Korean auto manufacturer, are among the region's success stories. There are certainly other large conglomerates, but many are still subcontracting to multinationals, such as the big Hong Kong and Taiwanese manufacturers, rather than brand owners themselves.

The halal industry offers some insight into the issues for local firms given that a halal-certified product has the potential to appeal to Muslim consumers around the world as long as it is a relatively generic product, such as toothpaste, rather than a culturally specific product, like Maggi *chorba* soup.

Malaysia is a good candidate to develop such regional halal players given that the country has led the region in terms of developing its halal industries. The government was the first in Asia to actively promote the sector, establishing the Halal Industry Development Corporation in 2006 to coordinate the sector's development, as well as building Halal Park, an industrial park near Kuala Lumpur where companies can take advantage of ready-built factories and tax incentives. The country's halal-certification authority, Jakim, is also one of the region's most credible and therefore theoretically trusted by Muslims in any country.

Even so, multinationals account for 70 percent of Malaysia's halal food exports. Part of the challenge is trust. "I saw the local politics play out in Malaysia recently while attending a conference—Indonesians were saying privately they didn't trust Malaysian brands and Malaysians were saying much the same about Indonesian brands," says FleishmanHillard's Yusuf Hatia. "But if you are Colgate, for instance, then you are seen as a global brand, even if it is Colgate Malaysia that is producing the final product. The companies who suffer are the small-scale brands, such as a small Malaysian toothpaste brand."

So what will it take to develop Malaysia's halal industries and nurture the country's future multinationals? Zarina Nalla is an Associate Director of IA Consulting, a Malaysian consultancy, and also co-founder of the International Institute of Advanced Islamic Studies (IAIS), a creation of the country's former Prime Minister, Tun Abdullah Ahmad Badawi. A longtime advisor on Islamic policy issues in Malaysia, Nalla had only recently completed an extensive study of the country's halal industry and was familiar with the challenges faced by local firms.

"The industry still lacks international standards, so mistrust is an issue. Local food processors also spend too little on research and development in order to compete with the big brands. They also lack the scale to fill large orders when they do receive them," she said, offering a realistic view of the challenges.

Mamee is one of those Malaysian food brands that perhaps will make the transition. The firm is famous for its Mister Potato, Mamee Instant Noodle, and Corntoz brands, and the company's packaging and marketing material are comparable to those of any of the big multinational brands with their smart logos, bright colors, and fun websites. Mamee Instant Noodles, in particular, are popular across the region. Most importantly, the firm's products are all stamped with the credible Jakim logo certifying that they are halal. "It makes strategic sense for Malaysia to nurture brands such as Mamee," says Nalla.[2]

The East's rising demand for high-quality goods is creating new opportunities

The issue of trust is especially important, and not only for the halal industry. Multinationals enjoy a head start in this respect, as their products and services are assumed to be of an equivalent standard to those in the West, where health and safety regulations are usually stricter and legal repercussions greater. However, foreign companies are not immune to challenges, as demonstrated by a string of recent food scares, notably in China, where a state-run broadcaster criticized KFC over alleged improper use of antibiotics in chickens supplied by Chinese companies.[3] Still, such scares are uncommon for now.

Hong Kong's experience is a vivid example of how trust can generate dollars. The territory is routinely swamped by tourists from mainland China looking to buy milk powder, Chinese traditional medicines, or high-end watches and handbags on the assumption that products sold in the territory are more likely to be genuine. Hong Kong consumers after all enjoy stronger consumer rights, and the government protects and enforces intellectual property rights more robustly. Small-scale farmers in Hong Kong are even making a comeback as a result of worries about food security and the import of tainted products from mainland China.

Those fears create opportunities not only for multinationals and their big global platforms but also for smaller foreign companies producing high-quality niche goods. Select food-processing companies are enjoying strong sales growth as more affluent households in the East worry about food safety; shops in Hong Kong and Singapore, for instance, increasingly sell organic beef flown in from New Zealand or organic fruits and vegetables from America. Cosmetic companies are similarly finding opportunities as online marketplaces in China, for example, offer plant-based cosmetic products from Japan and Germany.

Zip Industries, an Australian water filtration company, is another that has benefited from the trend. The company visited China in the early 2000s to explore prospects for manufacturing in the country, but decided against it and has since continued to manufacture in Australia at a higher price. That might have played against them in the early years but not anymore, as customers are prepared to pay for quality. After all, water filtration products are only worth buying if they actually work properly. And the fact that Zip's products are still "Made in Australia" provides customers with greater confidence.

Of course, there is still room for local competitors to provide a "just-good-enough" but lower-quality alternative that will appeal to the region's mass market that can't yet afford to pay for foreign imports. Nevertheless, the segment of the market that is able to pay is growing, and companies are spending considerable money on educating consumers in the value of quality. The growing number of returnees who have studied or worked abroad where they have been exposed to foreign goods, such as organic beef or water filtration, are also an increasingly important source of demand.

Multinationals will need to better balance global platforms with local autonomy

The challenge then is finding the right balance between matching a global product with local tastes. This is largely a people problem, as companies must find professional staff who understand what it means to be a global brand yet at the same time are also still in touch with local consumers, not just a globalized elite.

Take Sony Entertainment's relationship with the Indian Premier League. The fact that Michael Lynton, the company's CEO and an American national, grew up in Europe and understood cricket was critical to the firm's making such a big bet on a non-American sport in a foreign country. Equally, Man Jit Singh, the company's India CEO, had spent 30 years living in Los Angeles and watching LA Lakers games before returning to Mumbai to play a key role in the league's transformation—complete with the same cheerleaders seen at a typical NBA game.

The challenges also lie deeper than just global or country business heads. In order to compete with increasingly robust local competitors, multinationals and other foreign companies will need to acquire better insights into local tastes, and that means trusting local staff. In this, big companies are at a disadvantage as they struggle to find the right balance between local autonomy with global businesses and as some maintain rigid control over the local office while others provide more slack, to the point where the local office becomes a distinct subsidiary, even listed locally.

The fact that Honeywell's China-based engineers are producing products in competition with European colleagues is a case in point.[4]

And they aren't the only firm. In the spring of 2013, the *Wall Street Journal* reported that General Electric, an American multinational conglomerate, had won a contract to supply Indonesia's railroad operator with 100 locomotives. But only barely. "We had a close call," Stuart Dean, the conglomerate's Southeast Asia CEO, was quoted as saying. "Historically, we've taken global solutions and sold them all over the world. But we're competing with local companies, and need to fine-tune our strategies."

Western Union is another good example of a global firm acting locally. The company tied up with Indian megastar Shahrukh Khan's science fiction film *Ra.One* to promote the company's services even as it sponsored telescopes in mosques across India to help worshippers see the new moon signaling the start of the Eid holiday. They weren't the only multinational prepared to take a punt on the often complicated subject of religion after McDonald's in Indonesia took to wrapping the company's golden arches by day and then unwrapping them at night to signal an end to the fast.

Unilever is also a good example of a multinational with a global product but a distinct local business. The Anglo-Dutch multinational consumer goods company has been present in Indonesia since 1888 and has been listed on the local stock exchange for almost 30 years. To many, Unilever Indonesia is a local company. It is much the same for Hindustan Unilever, which has been in India since 1933 and is also listed on the stock exchange. Of course, the multinational has benefited from its fortuitous early investments in both countries, but the company's success also underscores the value of local autonomy for companies targeting local tastes.

Jonathan Bonsey is a 30-year veteran of Asia and owner of one of the region's leading design brand companies. He offered some sensible advice when we met over lunch in Singapore. "I would identify your core competence and then re-imagine it for the local market. Keep it simple, direct, and tailored to local tastes."[5] That message is especially important for new entrants to the region, as they are likely to find the competition from local, regional, and international firms stiff, meaning there is less time to build brand loyalty. Keeping it simple but sensitive to local tastes is a good place to start.

The East's holidays and religious festivals are creating new consumer cycles

Providing local units with greater autonomy will certainly help foreign companies better align themselves with the East's different consumer cycles, which are many and mixed. In the 1980s, the West still accounted for 50 percent of global consumption, meaning that Christmas was the largest sales period of the year and the time when the bulk of advertising and promotional budgets were spent. But the East's share of consumption has since risen to 20 percent of the global total, and little of that is spent during the Christmas period, but rather during the key Chinese, Hindu, Muslim, and other religious or ethnic festivals.

China, Hong Kong, Taiwan, and Singapore shut down during the Lunar New Year festival, the holiday floating around January and February. In Hong Kong, the change is especially evident as Christmas holiday decorations are taken down and replaced soon after by Lunar New Year versions. The commercial impact is evident, with Hong Kong's retail sales enjoying "Christmas-like" strength during the first month of the year, buoyed partly by an influx of 750,000 mainland Chinese tourists, equivalent to 10 percent of the city's population, during the nearly weeklong holiday.

The effect is much the same in India during the Diwali festival that falls sometime during October and November. Households spend heavily on gold and silver items, clothing, and household appliances during the holiday. Bonuses are paid out to public servants and other employees, further fueling spending among households who use the extra cash to buy big-ticket items. The festival's effect on gold demand is strong enough to cause precious-metal traders thousands of miles away in London to talk of a "Diwali effect" when speaking to the *Financial Times* and other international financial dailies.

Given that it affects so many countries across the region, it is the Muslim holiday at the end of Ramadan that has the most pronounced impact on the East. And while many foreign companies are reluctant to tie themselves to a religious festival, the opportunities are nonetheless significant. In India, Bollywood superstar Salman Khan traditionally releases a movie during the Eid festival to celebrate the end of the Ramadan period, much as Hollywood releases blockbusters ahead of Christmas. It's a much-awaited event for fans, and Khan inevitably dominates the box office during the Muslim holiday.

In Indonesia, rock bands release songs for the Islamic holy month. For instance, Ungu, an Indonesian megaband, plays hard rock but isn't shy about linking itself to Ramadan. In 2006, the band released an album to celebrate Ramadan, reportedly selling 150,000 copies in 15 days. The band has even deliberately toured Hong Kong during Ramadan, singing to stadiums packed with Indonesian domestic helpers. It's tough to see a performer such as the American pop star Taylor Swift using the same channels to sell to the world's fourth most populous country, and yet it's also a missed sales opportunity.

A "China + 1" strategy hedges overexposure to the region's giant

For much of the past decade, China was the only topic of conversation. I used to take slides full of talking points on the region's other countries—India, Malaysia, Thailand—into meetings, but inevitably the discussion would return to China and stay there. And yet, that's finally starting to change.

The change is best described as the "China + 1" strategy. It is a buzzword most popularly used in the sourcing industry and gradually gaining wider acceptance. The term implies overexposure to China. The country remains the East's biggest opportunity, but after more than a decade of pouring resources into China, many companies are over-reliant on the country either as a source of goods or as a place to sell goods. And that puts them at risk in the event of a major disruption, such as after a rise in production costs, a protectionist shift in policy, or the emergence of local competitors.

Foreign sourcing companies are especially sensitive to the risks. Many are dangerously exposed, importing 80 percent or more of their total goods from China. Rising wages and other costs are a threat, but so are worries of a trade war between China and the West. The European Union's decision to impose tariffs as high as 73 percent on Chinese ceramic tiles in 2011, for instance, was a clear example of the risk.[6] "We were importing 90 percent of our tiles from China. But overnight it became cheaper for us to produce in Italy," one European sourcing agent on the fringes of a conference in Hong Kong told me.

These concerns are often as important as relative differences in wages, land, or electricity prices. Even if the cost differential is not significant, simply building an additional plant near Jakarta rather than near Guangzhou can protect against a range of risks. Indeed, the driving purpose of building that factory might simply be to reduce China's share of production from 80 percent to 60 percent, which is no different from how sourcing companies look to share their orders across a number of factories in China itself rather than being reliant on a single factory in Dongguan in southern Guangdong province.

For the retail sector, the rise of local competitors can be equally important. China might be one of the world's great consumer opportunities, but it is also a hothouse for entrepreneurs who are looking to sell to those same consumers. Growing sales in other countries where local competition is less fierce, such as in Indonesia, might offer a diversification strategy in the event that sales in China take a hit. Of course, this doesn't mean ignoring China altogether, but rather growing sales in other countries and so reducing a firm's relative exposure to China.

The East's disruptive forces will create opportunities, not just threats

The potential for resource disruption is not just tied to China. Metito's Rami Ghandour tells a story about traveling through the Japanese town of Hakone, a short distance from Tokyo and famous for its hot springs. "I was in the city's main train station and see Masafi water for sale in a vending machine," he says, referring to the branded water bottled in the UAE's hilly eastern border with Oman. "Why is a water-poor country exporting to a water-rich country?" His story neatly illustrates how much of the region seems to overlook looming resource shortages and the resulting significant potential for commercial disruption.

Consider Hong Kong, where water consumption is among the world's highest, a situation inconsistent with the fact that neighboring Guangdong province, from which Hong Kong imports much of its water, is targeting a reduction in water consumption over the coming decades. In fact, Hong Kong continued to receive an uninterrupted supply of water in 2009 after Guangdong was hit by the province's worst drought in 60 years, which affected large tracts of farmland and left fishing boats beached on riverbeds. Ensuring that the city has an adequate water supply is not just about economics but also arguably about politics.

Even so, Hong Kong's water prices are among the lowest in the world, and it seems inevitable that water prices must rise sharply, putting the working class under further financial stress. If the increases are absorbed by subsidies, then the additional spending leaves the government with less cash for other public services. The opportunities for spending on water-efficient appliances are significant, however, with households likely to replace ageing washing machines with newer and more efficient models or to switch to showerheads that restrict water pressure.

Other disruptions include the potential impact of floods and other natural disasters on supply chains. The impact of Japan's devastating tsunami in 2011 and Thailand's protracted floods the same year certainly had many reviewing the vulnerability of their supply chains. Meanwhile, Indonesia offers a low-cost alternative to China, yet the country's coastline is also prone to natural risks, complicating the equation. The increasingly complex nature of the region's supply chains also means that even if a company's factory is not affected, suppliers might be, and production would still be halted.

Possible disruptions aren't limited to resource shortages or natural disasters. Political risks are growing again across the region as tensions emerge between China and Japan over territorial claims in the South China Sea with implications for business. Some 52 percent of Japanese firms are looking to expand in China, based on surveys by Japan's external trade agency. By contrast, the figure is a far higher 78 percent for Indonesia, and even higher again for Laos, Bangladesh, and India, in spite of the fact that all these countries are smaller markets with often bigger issues.[7]

The spread of e-commerce offers new ways to tap the Muslim consumer

The ties between the Muslim consumer and the e-commerce sector are also among the region's more persuasive. The region's Muslim population is on average five years younger than its non-Muslim population, and young people are typically early adopters of new technology, so it's perhaps no surprise that the share of people using the Internet is high in the Muslim world, with countries such as Malaysia, Saudi Arabia, Lebanon, and Turkey all enjoying high usage rates. Indeed, it was online youth activists that were central to the social protests across the region during the past few years.

The number of mobile apps is also growing, in part supported by Muslim developers in America and Europe. Over time, mobile apps will form a central part of the online halal business in the East. However, for now there is a greater preference among Muslim consumers in the region to browse websites.

HijUp.com is one of those sites that is benefiting from Indonesia's growing e-commerce sales. The site sells fashion for Muslim women, mainly hijabs covering the head and neck. The site features attractive Indonesian models wearing the company's latest designs and also offers a range of accessories such as bracelets, rings, and sunglasses. *Be Fabulous with HijUp* was splashed across the home page next to an offer of a free Ramadan diary for all new customers and an embedded video that featured the company's recent HijUp Model Competition. The site isn't shy about putting young Indonesian Muslim women in the public eye.

I tested out their delivery service with a family friend, a fashionable Muslim mother, in Jakarta. We ordered a Paris Classic scarf in blue for $9 plus shipping, and the box duly arrived a few days later, delivered by local courier, the scarf wrapped neatly in an attractively designed light-blue fabric bag.

The ability to ship goods anywhere in Indonesia also allowed HijUp to tap into the country's population of 115 million women living outside of Jakarta, where the company is based, much the same as Glamour-Sales in Shanghai is able to sell more than 30 percent of its products to third- and fourth-tier cities. Moreover, HijUp's online business model helps to overcome the challenge of selling to women in a country where the typical household has two to three children, so that many mothers may be stuck at home and unable to spend a few hours shopping in town, as compared to China's single-child families.

Impressed by HijUp's service, I reached out to their CEO, Diajeng Lestari, to ask about the business model. "At HijUp, we have one million visitors a year of which 5 percent turn into customers," she said. "We also have more than 10 million views on our YouTube channel." I asked about the challenges of selling to multiple midsized cities. "We see this as an opportunity. In Europe or the United States, there are [a] lot of wealthy cities where traditional retail is run well and generally profitable. In Indonesia, that's often not the case. That's why there is an opportunity for Indonesian e-commerce players to dominate."[8]

The tie-up between e-commerce and other innovative technologies will further extend the opportunities to both local and foreign companies. For instance, the combination of e-commerce platforms such as HijUp or Glamour-Sales, when combined with the possibilities of branchless payment transactions conducted through mobile phones, opens up those parts of the economy that are even less accessible, such as a Muslim mother in a largely rural Indonesian city or a migrant worker in a remote Chinese town, not to mention the urban poor, such as those in Cairo or Mumbai, who may not be plugged into the local economy in spite of living in giant cities.

The East's large and growing cities will accelerate the adoption of e-commerce

It is the marriage of e-commerce and urbanization that is especially explosive. The region's consumer opportunities are no longer limited to just a few major cities, but instead extend to some 325 midsized cities across the East with populations greater than 750,000, more than twice the number of such cities in the West.

Given the new technologies available, there is no reason for the East to follow the same development pattern as the West. And I would be surprised if the region's consumer product companies followed the same physical store model as they did in the West. Already there are signs in China that shoppers are increasingly using stores as places to inspect goods, rather than to buy. The sheer number of cities is likely to accelerate this trend as only the largest and most successful brands, such as Dyson, the British appliance retailer, are able to open outlets in multiple countries and cities.

Other forces will accelerate the change. The adoption of smartphone devices across the region is among the more powerful. Take Tencent, one of China's largest online media companies, and WeChat, the company's mobile text messaging application with over 300 million users in China. WeChat recently added a new function to the device that allows shoppers to scan a barcode and compare prices across multiple online sites. Given how regularly urban Chinese are already shopping online, it's tough to see how retailers selling everyday products can compete unless they offer the lowest possible price.

Consider also how a major virus outbreak might affect the way the region shops. In 2003, households still had to physically buy food and clothing from stores. Today, many are already buying online from grocery and apparel stores, such as China's No. 1 Store selling everything from seafood to suits with goods delivered in two days or the same day in Shanghai. Sure, a virus outbreak is only a temporary phenomenon, but it might have a permanent effect on the way the region shops as households not yet regularly buying online are incentivized to do so as they worry about their family's health.

The combination of e-commerce and the region's many cities may also change the way parcels are delivered. Amazon, the giant American online retailer, offers a growing network of delivery lockers across many of America's biggest cities, allowing customers to collect their goods by punching in a code. The East is well suited to a similar service, especially in already gridlocked cities, therefore reducing the need to build more roads. And if companies do not build purpose-designed lockers, local mom-and-pop stores may offer informal services as an extra source of cash.

In the West, most products are still displayed in large networks of retail chains and department stores. Might the East simply leapfrog this model and build only display stores that generate their revenues by selling inventory solutions to sellers or parcel retrieval to buyers? I am reminded of the vast exhibition halls in the Chinese coastal city of Yiwu where wholesalers display single items of their products in permanent stands for inspection by buyers. Inventories are held elsewhere and shipped on order. Yiwu's wholesalers have organized to arrange trade shows abroad. Why not a series of Yiwu outlets?

The most important point is that the unique conditions of selling to Asia's many but dispersed consumers, when mixed with the rapid uptake of online sales, are likely to produce innovative solutions to today's challenges, and the region is unlikely to follow in the same trajectory as the West. As KPMG's Edge Zarrella says, it's not enough to look for a Chinese Steve Jobs or an Indonesian Jeff Bezos. The region is already innovating in how it buys goods, so foreign companies must be prepared to adapt to innovative business models and sales channels to tap into the region's consumers.

Myanmar's re-emergence illustrates how quickly major commercial assumptions can change

The speed of change across the East is dazzling. E-commerce is just one of the more exciting developments. But sometimes the change is more old-school. Myanmar's re-emergence, for instance, illustrates how quickly opportunities can recalibrate across the region as disruptions spill between countries.

"Myanmar's quality is terrific," says Lewis Leung, founder of PERM, a Hong Kong–based management and investment consultancy. Leung spent several years living in Yangon, the former capital of Myanmar, in the late 1990s as a factory manager before leaving to set up a number of factories in Vietnam and China and then finally returning to Hong Kong. We met for lunch at Hong Kong's Foreign Correspondents Club, an apt location given that the club is based in an old colonial building resembling those that populate much of Yangon. I ask how he compares Myanmar and Vietnam. "Myanmar is another Vietnam," he states confidently. "Similar size. Similar quality."[9]

The result is yet another shift in the region's manufacturing patterns as retailers source from yet another country. Japanese firms in particular may see the country as a hedge against their large operations in China. Vietnam is a potential loser. But even so, size matters. China's apparel exports are 20 times those of Vietnam, and Myanmar is equally likely to remain a niche player, more impacted by changes in China's production. Indeed, Myanmar's total youth population of 13 million is not much larger than the total number of migrant workers who leave from Guangzhou's main station each Lunar New Year.

But it's not only about export manufacturing. Thailand relies heavily on a cheap Burmese workforce with some 1.1 million documented workers and potentially several million undocumented.[10] Chances are that many will return home, lured by new job opportunities, thus adding to Thailand's already severe labor shortages. That's good news for the country's retailers as wage increases support more spending. It might also accelerate the development of midsized towns as factories and businesses alike are forced to chase labor across the country, much as China's own midsized cities are developing.

Myanmar's reintegration into the region's manufacturing base and its growing consumer market will also impact the region's transport linkages. Development banks and governments are already spending to expand transport corridors, such as those running north to south to connect China, Laos, and Thailand, or those running east to west to link Vietnam, Thailand, and Myanmar. The idea of a European Union–style network of roads and transport companies is still decades away, but momentum is definitely in the region's favor as a result of market forces and the arrival of the ASEAN Economic Community.

SALMAN TARIQ IS THE FUTURE OF THE EAST'S GROWTH, AND ALSO ITS complexity. Born in the Pakistani city of Lahore, he later studied at Hong Kong University and today works in the Hong Kong office of Al-Iradah Kizuna Consulting, assisting mainly Japanese companies targeting the region's halal markets. Tariq's latest project involves assisting a 100-year-old Japanese confectionery company with plans to sell its sweets in Malaysia. The company was looking for help in positioning its product for the Muslim consumer, starting with Malaysia, and Tariq was providing a preliminary market study.

"We've seen Japanese companies wanting to hedge their exposure to China because of political tensions," he says over lunch at the Suzuki Café in Hong Kong's upcoming Sheng Wan district. "That's encouraging many to look at Southeast Asia's Muslim markets for the first time. Before it was all too hard. But they now have incentive."[11]

Tariq is also 24 years old and periodically checks his Samsung smartphone as we chat. Even if parts of the East are ageing, the region's average age is just 26 years, some 14 years younger than that in the West. The region's youth are also online and increasingly buying online. The East's rise is about the rise of economies based not only on different cultures but also on different generations; much as China's youth are fueling the country's e-commerce sales and forcing change on the logistics sector, India's youth are contributing to the rise of a faster-paced cricket game through the Indian Premier League and impacting the global game in turn.

From outside the region, the rapid pace of change can appear overwhelming at times. But that simply calls for more thoughtful consideration of the market opportunities and business structures that will drive a successful entry or expansion strategy. Recognizing that mental maps are increasingly challenging also means that it is tough to rely on a single individual to drive a successful strategy across the region. Many leading firms already have business councils or leadership groups in place to exchange ideas between countries and sectors and thus build a collective mental map.

Much like the historical Silk Road, capturing the commercial opportunities in the modern East is about making the most of the many complex daily interactions that take place between customers, businesses, and cities, even while recognizing the bigger structural trends that are driving the region in new and often surprising directions. This is a very different situation from that of the past 60 years when a single economy, the United States, was a major driver of global growth, and even Europe was unifying as a single market. Today's challenge is complexity and how to embrace it—and thus profit from the rise of a new East.

NOTES

Introduction

1. "Country Analysis: Saudi Arabia," US Energy Information Administration, February 26, 2013, http://www.eia.gov/countries/country-data.cfm?fips=sa.

Chapter 1: The Rise of the East's Middle Class

1. Hartono Jap, conversation with author, May 14, 2013.
2. Unilever Annual Report 2008 & 2012, http://www.unilever.com/investor relations/annual_reports/.
3. "Domestic Auto Market & Exim by Category," Association of Indonesian Automotive Industries, http://www.gaikindo.or.id/.
4. Author's calculations based on data sourced from *PovcalNET*, World Bank, http://iresearch.worldbank.org/PovcalNet/index.htm; *World Development Indicators*,WorldBank,http://data.worldbank.org/data-catalog/world-develop ment-indicators. Estimates of the middle class are notoriously tricky owing to the lack of reliable household income data in most emerging markets and the lack of cross-country comparable household income data. Household income can also vary significantly depending on the number of employed adults per family.
5. Author's calculations based on data sourced from multiple national statistical authorities.
6. "Motor Vehicles," *National Economic Accounts*, US Bureau of Economic Analysis, September 9, 2013, http://www.bea.gov/national/. Note that the US figures include autos and light trucks sales and so possibly overstate the numbers relative to the East, where distinguishing between the two categories is far harder.
7. Author's calculations based on data sourced from "Beauty Industry 2012 Outlook," Demeter Group, http://www.demetergroup.net/docs/whitepapers

/Demeter_Group_Beauty_Industry_2012_Outlook.pdf; "NationalEconomic Accounts," Bureau of Economic Analysis, US Department of Commerce, http://www.bea.gov/national/index.htm#gdp.

8. For the sake of simplicity in demonstrating the point, the model assumes a constant 5 percent change in nominal household consumption aside from China and Indonesia, where the estimates are 7 percent. However, more detailed projections would assume country-specific, or income-specific, percentages for growth of household consumption growth and share of household spending allocated to beauty products. As always with these models, China's figures can easily overwhelm other countries and, in this instance, account for roughly one-third of the total.

9. Author's calculations based on data sourced from "National Economic Accounts," Bureau of Economic Analysis, US Department of Commerce, http://www.bea.gov/national/index.htm#gdp; *World Development Indicators*, World Bank, http://data.worldbank.org/data-catalog/world-development -indicators.

10. Author's calculations based on data sourced from "China Statistical Yearbook 2012," National Bureau of Statistics of China, 2012. The national figures are supplemented by data sourced from multiple local Chinese statistical authorities, typically annual statistical yearbooks where possible. Note that the data are not adjusted for purchasing power parity.

11. Author's calculations based on data sourced from "Expenditure for Consumption of Indonesia by Province: National Socioeconomic Survey 2012," Statistics Indonesia, September 2012. Note that the data are not adjusted for purchasing power parity.

12. *World Urbanization Prospects: The 2011 Revision*, Department of Economic and Social Affairs, Population Division, Population Estimates and Projections Section, United Nations, http://esa.un.org/unup/.

13. Helmuth Hennig, conversation with author, April 30, 2013.

14. Thibault Villet, conversation with author, July 8, 2013.

15. Edge Zarrella, conversation with author, April 18, 2013.

16. Author's estimate.

17. Company website, http://www.sf-express.com.

18. "Internet Usage in Asia," Miniwatts Marketing Group, http://www .internetworldstats.com/stats.htm; "World Telecommunication/ICT Indicators Database 2013," 17th ed., ITU, June 17, 2013, http://www.itu.int/en /ITU-D/Statistics/Pages/publications/wtid.aspx; "Mobile Phone Penetration in Indonesia Triples in Five Years," Nielsen Company, February 23, 2011; "Southeast Asia's Mobile Phones Market Grew by 24 Percent in Volume over the Last 12 Months," GfK, September 17, 2012, http://www.gfk.com/news

-and-events/press-room/press-releases/pages/gfk asia–southeast asias mobile phones market grew by 24 percent in volume over the last 12 months.aspx.

19. Wasant Pothipimpanon, conversation with author, July 11, 2013.
20. National Statistical Office of Thailand, http://web.nso.go.th/.
21. Author's calculations based on data sourced from "Quarterly Report of Wages and Payroll Statistics," Hong Kong Census and Statistics Department, March 2013, http://www.censtatd.gov.hk/hkstat/sub/sp210 .jsp?productCode=B1050009.
22. UN Comtrade database, http://comtrade.un.org/db/.

Chapter 2: The End of "Made in China"?

1. "Guangdong qunian xinzeng jiuye 167 wanren yuji chunjie qianhou wu yonggonghuang" (1.67 million new jobs added in Guangdong last year, no labor shortage seen around Chinese New Year), *Zhongguo Xinwen Shi*, January 28, 2013.
2. Deng Yuanming, conversation with author, February 17, 2011.
3. "World Population Prospects: The 2012 Revision," Department of Economic and Social Affairs, Population Division, Population Estimates and Projections Section, United Nations, http://esa.un.org/wpp/.
4. "The 22nd Survey of Investment Related Costs in Asia and Oceania: FY 2011 Survey," Japan External Trade Organization (JETRO), April 2012, http://www.jetro.go.jp/en/reports/survey/biz/.
5. Richard Thomas, conversation with author, September 11, 2013.
6. UN Comtrade database, http://comtrade.un.org/db/.
7. Hoang Anh Dung, conversation with author, July 4, 2013.
8. "Major Shippers Report," Office of Textiles & Apparel, International Trade Administration, US Department of Commerce, July 2013, http://otexa.ita .doc.gov/catss.htm.
9. "The 22nd Survey of Investment Related Costs in Asia and Oceania: FY 2011 Survey," JETRO.
10. Neale O'Connor, conversation with author, August 9, 2013.
11. Gideon Milstein, conversation with author, April 19, 2012, and email exchange with author, August 20, 2013.
12. Sarah Monks, *Toy Town* (Hong Kong: PPL Co. Ltd., 2011), 241–243.
13. Ibid.
14. Ringo Mak, conversation with author, April 19, 2013.
15. Simon Kitchen, email exchange with author, September 11, 2013, and conversation with author, September 24, 2013.
16. Mahmoud al Haddad, conversation with author, November 24, 2012.

17. "Haixin Aiji kong tiao sheng chan ji di jian cheng tou chan" (Hisense's new air-conditioner production facilities in Egypt come on stream), *Sina News,* February 1, 2010.

18. "World Population Prospects: The 2012 Revision," Department of Economic and Social Affairs, Population Division, Population Estimates and Projections Section, United Nations, http://esa.un.org/wpp/.

19. UN Comtrade database, http://comtrade.un.org/db/.

Chapter 3: Tapping into the Muslim Market

1. The Zabihah app states that Pret A Manger's Hong Kong main office verbally confirms that all chicken is halal. The app relies on users to obtain such confirmations.

2. Author's calculations based on data sourced from "The Future of the Global Muslim Population: Projections for 2010–2030," Pew Research Centre, January 27, 2011, http://www.pewforum.org/2011/01/27/the-future-of-the -global-muslim-population/.

3. "World Population Prospects: The 2012 Revision," Department of Economic and Social Affairs, Population Division, Population Estimates and Projections Section, United Nations, http://esa.un.org/wpp/.

4. Author's calculations based on data sourced from "World Economic Outlook Database: April 2013," International Monetary Fund, http://www.imf.org /external/pubs/ft/weo/2013/01/weodata/index.aspx.

5. "Statistical Review of World Energy 2013," *BP,* http://www.bp.com/en /global/corporate/about-bp/statistical-review-of-world-energy-2013.html.

6. Yusuf Hatia, conversation with author, June 28, 2013.

7. "World Population Prospects: The 2012 Revision," Department of Economic and Social Affairs, Population Division, Population Estimates and Projections Section, United Nations, http://esa.un.org/wpp/.

8. "Nestlé expands its halal presence with the launch of its 'Flavours of Ramadan' range throughout the Islamic fasting period," Nestlé, August 23, 2010, http://www.nestle.com/Media/NewsAndFeatures/Nestle-expands -halal-presence-during-Ramadan.

9. "KFC Forced to Ditch Halal-only Menus after Disappointing Sales," *Daily Mail,* June 25, 2010.

10. Alwi Aidid, conversation with author, March 12, 2010, and email exchange with author, September 5, 2013.

11. Kenneth Mays, conversation with author, July 2, 2013.

12. Mohammed Al-Sudairi, *China in the Eyes of the Saudi Media,* Gulf Research Center, February 2013.

13. "Religion in England and Wales: 2011 Census," Office for National Statistics, December 11, 2012, http://www.ons.gov.uk/ons/rel/census/2011-census/key -statistics-for-local-authorities-in-england-and-wales/rpt-religion.html.

14. Omar Shaikh, conversation with author, May 31, 2013, and email exchange with author, August 15, 2013.

15. "Global Halal Cosmetics Market Booms," *AFP*, May 5, 2010.

16. Author's calculations based on data sourced from *World Bank Development Indicators*, World Bank; "The Future of the Global Muslim Population: Projections for 2010–2030," Pew Research Centre, January 27, 2011.

Chapter 4: Bollywood Stars and Indonesian Punk Rock

1. Jahil Thakkar, phone interview by author, June 20, 2013.

2. Jahil Thakkar, email exchange with author, September 17, 2013.

3. "The Power of a Billion: Realizing the Indian Dream," FICCI-KPMG, 2013, http://www.kpmg.com/in/en/issuesandinsights/articlespublications/pages /ficci-13.aspx.

4. Ibid.

5. Tanaaz Bhatia, conversation with author, June 28, 2013.

6. "Theatrical Market Statistics 2012," Motion Picture Association of America, 2012, http://www.mpaa.org/policy/industry.

7. Jason Dietz, "Metacritic's 4th Annual Movie Studio Report Card," Metacritic, February 12, 2013, http://www.metacritic.com/feature/film -studio-rankings-2013.

8. Ibid., February 6, 2012.

9. "Theatrical Market Statistics 2012," Motion Picture Association of America, 2012; "China Film Biz under Pressure," *Variety Media*, December 20, 2012.

10. Author's calculations based on data sourced from Box Office Mojo, http://www.boxofficemojo.com/movies/?id=expendables2.htm; http://www .boxofficemojo.com/movies/?id=lincoln.htm.

11. Robert Cain, phone interview by author, July 16, 2013.

12. Raymond Zhou, phone interview by author, August 1, 2013.

13. Zhong Ying Xing Mei's company website, http://www.zyxmmovie.com/.

14. Tony Ngai, conversation with author, August 1, 2013.

15. Sunil Gavaskar, *Sunny Days: Sunil Gavaskar's Own Story* (New Delhi: Rupa & Co., 2011).

16. "The World's 100 Highest-Paid Athletes: #51 Sachin Tendulkar," *Forbes*, May 6, 2013.

17. Man Jit Singh, conversation with author, June 26, 2013.

18. "Matt Prior Says IPL May Cause England Player Tensions," *BBC Sport*, February 14, 2013.
19. Cherry Leong, conversation with author, April 29, 2013.
20. Wendi Putranto, conversation with author, May 15, 2013.
21. "Smartphone Penetration Doubles in Indonesia," eMarketer, August 3, 2013.
22. "Internet Usage in Asia," Usage and Population Statistics, Inter World Stats, http://www.internetworldstats.com/stats3.htm.

Chapter 5: China Goes Global, Again

1. Tony Shi, conversation with author, December 22, 2013.
2. "Zhongguo qiye haiwai touzi ji jingying zhuangqing diaocha baogao" (Chinese Enterprises Overseas Investment and Operating Conditions Survey Report), *Zhongguo Guoji Maoyi Cujin Weiyuanhui*, April 2012.
3. "2013 nian shangban nian quanguo dianying piaofang tongji" (First-Half 2013 National Box Office Statistics), *The State Administration of Radio and Film Television*, July 11, 2013.
4. Author's calculations based on a range of data sources, including the People's Bank of China, China Banking Regulatory Commission, National Bureau of Statistics of China, Asian Development Bank, and official media quotes.
5. Tony Shi, phone interview by author, August 6, 2013.
6. "Wizaara al tarbiya taqqara bi fashal tujriba isnaad tanfeez mushaari`a madrasiya al sharika al Sineeya wa tahammalha masu'liya t'akhir tanfeez-iha" (The Ministry of Education Recognizes the Failure of the Experience of Assigning the Implementation of School Projects for Chinese Companies Who Bear Responsibility for Delay in Implementation)," *Al Arqaan*, August 5, 2013.
7. Paul Speltz, conversation with author, January 14, 2013.
8. "Hui jia de gu shi–zhongguo zai libiya ren yuan che li fan xiang ji" (Coming Home—the Story of Chinese Overseas Workers Pulling out from Libya), *Nanjing Longhoo.net*, March 5, 2011.
9. "2013 nian shangban nian wuguo duiwai laowu hezuo yewu jianming tong ji" (Concise Statistics on China's Foreign Labor Service Cooperation for First Half of 2013), *Ministry of Commerce, People's Republic of China*, July 1, 2013.
10. "Algerian-Chinese Clash an Isolated Case—Chinese Ambassador," *BBC Monitoring Asia Pacific*, August 7, 2009.
11. "Transforming Wartime Contracting: Controlling Costs, Reducing Risks," Commission on Wartime Contracting in Iraq and Afghanistan, August 2011;

Amy Belasco, "Troop Levels in the Afghan and Iraq Wars, FY2001–FY2012: Cost and Other Potential Issues," Congressional Research Service, July 2, 2009.

12. "Fengxian quanqiuhua zhongde minshi anquan: zhongguo haiwai quanyi de feizhengfu de anquanbaowei" (Civil Security in Risk Globalization: China's Overseas Interests and Non-Government Forces), *Zhongguo Gonggong Anquan: Xueshuban* 2, no. 23 (2011).

13. Brian Spegele and Nicholas Bariyo, "Sudan Says Some Chinese Workers Freed; Doubts Remain," *Wall Street Journal*, January 31, 2012.

14. Paul Speltz, conversation with author, January 14, 2013.

15. "World Investment Prospects Survey 2012–2014", UNCTAD, 2012, http://www.unctad.org/en/PublicationsLibrary/webdiaeia2012d21_en.pdf.

Chapter 6: Small Trucks and Big Planes

1. Matthew Flynn, *Water Margin: Hong Kong's Links to the Sea* (Hong Kong: Flynn Books, 2012).

2. "International Transactions, by Area," Bureau of Economic Analysis, US Department of Commerce, http://www.bea.gov/iTable/iTable.cfm?ReqID=6&step=1#reqid=6&step=1&isuri=1; Statistics Database, World Trade Organization, http://stat.wto.org/Home/WSDBHome.aspx?Language=E.

3. Angkana Songvejkasem, conversation with author, July 3, 2013.

4. Glenda Korporaal, "Exporters Risk Missing Boat in Asia, Warns Linfox Boss Peter Fox," *The Australian*, March 2, 2013.

5. Craig Hope-Johnstone, conversation with author, July 2, 2013.

6. Colin Airdrie, conversation with author, January 8, 2013, and email exchange with author, September 11, 2013.

7. Yared Desta, conversation with author, August 2, 2013.

8. Ka-Kin Cheuk, *Indians in the Chinese Textile City: Middleman Traders in Upgrading Economy*, Draft for Emerging Scholars Symposium, Indian China Institute, New School for Social Research, April 2012, http://indiachinainstitute.org/2012/04/23/emerging-scholars-2012-papers/.

9. "June 17, 1947: Pan Am Launches 'Round-the-World Service," *Wired*, June 17, 2009.

10. "Zhengque duidai teshu qingkuang xia de chaojin" (Correctly Dealing with the Special Circumstances of the Haj), State Administration for Religious Affairs of P.R.C., August 2, 2013.

11. "Hotel Benchmarks Survey Reports (2007–2013)," Ernst & Young, 2013, http://www.ey.com/EM/en/Industries/Real-Estate/REHL_Library; "Dubai Hotel Room & Apartment Flat Occupancy (2002–2011)," Department of

Tourism and Commerce Marketing, 2011, http://www.dubaitourism.ae/en /trade-resources/statistics/hotel-statistics.

Chapter 7: The East's Uncertain Urban Future

1. "World Population Prospects: The 2012 Revision," Department of Economic and Social Affairs, Population Division, Population Estimates and Projections Section, United Nations, http://esa.un.org/wpp/.
2. Ernst Zimmermann, conversation with author, January 12, 2011, and February 5, 2013.
3. The $1.75 trillion (10.7 trillion yuan) figure is based on an audit by the State Auditor in June 2011. However, the government was in the process of another audit in autumn 2013 and a new figure is expected after publication of the book.
4. "Housing Stock, Amenities & Assets in Slums: Census 2011," Census of India, 2011, http://www.censusindia.gov.in/2011census/hlo/Slum_table/Slum _table.html.
5. Ibid.
6. Aseena Viccajee, conversation with author, June 27, 2013.
7. David Sims, *Understanding Cairo: The Logic of a City Out of Control* (Cairo: American University in Cairo Press, 2010), 95.
8. M-Pesa, the mobile-phone-based money transfer in Kenya and Tanzania, is the best example of this business.
9. Ahmed Dermish, Christoph Kneiding, Paul Leishman, and Ignacio Mas, "Branchless and Mobile Banking Solutions for the Poor: A Survey of the Literature," *Innovations* 6, no. 4 (Fall 2011).
10. Mike Every, phone interview by author, November 20, 2011.
11. Somchai, conversation with author, July 4, 2013.
12. Susan Hanson, Robert Nicholls, N. Ranger, S. Hallegatte, J. Corfee-Morlot, C. Herweijer, and J. Chateau, "A Global Ranking of Port Cities with High Exposure to Climate Extremes," *Climatic Change* 104 (2011): 89–111.
13. "The World Bank Supports Thailand's Post-Floods Recovery Effort," World Bank, December 13, 2011, http://www.worldbank.org/en/news/ feature/2011/12/13/world-bank-supports-thailands-post-floods-recovery-effort.

Chapter 8: A Water and Energy Nexus

1. Rami Ghandour, conversation with author, June 11, 2013.
2. AQUASTAT database, Food and Agriculture Organization of the United Nations, http://www.fao.org/nr/water/aquastat/main/index.stm.

3. Samer Yousef, conversation with author, June 11, 2013.

4. "Survey Shows Hong Kongers Take 14-minute Long Showers: More than 20,000 Students and 4,000 Citizens Help Curb CO_2 Emissions Via '5-minute Shower Challenge,'" *Green Power*, March 19, 2013, www .greenpower.org.hk/html/download/190313_5min_Eng.doc.

5. To be fair, consumers aren't the biggest drinkers of water. The water we use in cities—for drinking, washing clothes, or running air conditioning— accounts for just 11 percent of global water consumption. The real culprits are agriculture, which accounts for 70 percent of consumption, and industry, which consumes another 19 percent. See International Energy Agency, *World Energy Outlook 2012* (Paris: OECD, 2012), 502.

6. Glen Plumbridge, conversation with author, April 23, 2014, and July 22, 2013.

7. "China Statistical Yearbook: 2012," National Bureau of Statistics of China, 2012; "What is the Role of Coal in the United States?" US Energy Information Administration, August 16, 2013, http://www.eia.gov/energy_in_brief/article /role_coal_us.cfm.

8. Terry Foecke, conversation with author, August 7, 2013.

9. James Zhang, phone interview by author, August 20, 2013.

10. Jason Lo, conversation with author, July 8, 2013.

11. "Advantage America: The US-China Clean Energy Technology Trade Relationship in 2011," Pew Charitable Trust, March 6, 2013, http://www .pewenvironment.org/news-room/reports/advantage-america-the-us-china -clean-energy-technology-trade-relationship-in-2011-85899456253.

Conclusion

1. Industry changed for confidentiality.

2. Zarina Nalla, phone interview by author, July 31, 2013.

3. Colum Murphy, "KFC Criticized over Suppliers in China," *Wall Street Journal*, December 19, 2012.

4. Kathy Chu, "Western Firms Rethink Asia Approach," *Wall Street Journal*, March 11, 2013.

5. Jonathan Bonsey, conversation with author, March 1, 2013.

6. Jonathan Stearns, "China's Ceramic-Tile Exporters Face EU Tariffs as High as 73%," *Bloomberg News*, March 17, 2011.

7. "Survey of Japanese-Affiliated Companies in Asia and Oceania (FY 2012 Survey)," Japan External Trade Organization (JETRO), December 2012, http://www.jetro.go.jp/en/reports/survey/biz/.

8. Diajeng Lestari, email exchange with author, September 14, 2013.

9. Lewis Leung, conversation with author, August 12, 2013, and email exchange with author, September 10, 2013.
10. "Thailand Migration Report 2011," International Organization for Migration, 2011, www.un.or.th/documents/tmr-2011.pdf.
11. Salman Tariq, conversation with author, September 12, 2013.

INDEX